Doug Bell and Rhoda Robertson

TWO COOKS AND A SUITCASE

Scorpion Press, Edinburgh

FIRST EDITION NOVEMBER 2002
PUBLISHED BY SCORPION PRESS, EDINBURGH
30 UPPER GILMORE PLACE, EDINBURGH

COPYRIGHT © DOUGLAS BELL AND RHODA ROBERTSON
FOOD PHOTOGRAPHS COPYRIGHT © NEIL CAMMOCK
ALL RIGHTS RESERVED

No part of this book may be reproduced, stored in a retrieval system, or transmitted in Any form or by any other means, electronic, magnetic tape, mechanical, photocopying, recording or otherwise without prior permission of the publishers.

ISBN 0-9543979-0-8

Back and front cover design by George Miller
Back cover photography by Cecil Rimes
Book design and production by Minuteman Press (Edinburgh)
Text edited by John Aitchison
Pachuko Plaque text by Gordon Dobie
Food Photographs by Neil Cammock

Distributed by: Lupe Pintos Deli

24 Leven Street	313 Great Western Road
Edinburgh	Glasgow
EH3 9LJ	G4 9HR
Tel: 0131 228 6241	Tel: 0141 334 5444

www.lupepintos.com

This book is for

Vincent and Audrey

Acknowledgements

Thanks to every stallholder, shopkeeper, restaurateur and neighbourhood cook for recipes, cooking tips and general enthusiasm.

Special thanks to: Ken Vallante, Sharyn Vallante, Wayne, Linda and Lee in Boston. Kelly Keller, Steve, Ryan, Marcus, Cathy and Little Buddy in New Orleans. Hilary Richardson in Los Angeles and Lupe Pinto and family in Progresso.

A very special thanks to John Aitchison for editing pages of rantings into a compact story, to Liz Anderson and Gerry Tonner (www.smackvan.com) for fine tuning and George Miller for the best book cover.

Finally thanks to all our friends and family for eating our experiments.

CONTENTS

- Two Cooks And A Suitcase - The Story   *pages 5 - 24*
- Introduction To The Recipes   *page 25*
- The Basics - Cuisines' Explained   *page 26*
- Making A Roux   *page 27*
- Mexican Techniques - Garnish Tips, Using Chiles, Roasting and Preparing Vegetables and Spices.   *pages 27 - 29*
- The Tortilla And Masa Harina Guide - Home Made Corn Tortillas, Wheat Tortillas, Tamales.   *pages 30 - 33*
- Basic Recipes - Stocks, Sauces and Condiments   *pages 34 - 41*
- Soups   *pages 42 - 49*
- Starters - Antojitos   *pages 50 - 58*
- Fish & Seafood   *pages 59 - 70*
- Meat   *pages 71 - 86*
- Chicken   *pages 87 - 100*
- Cajun Side Dishes   *pages 101 - 112*
- Mexican Side Dishes   *pages 113 - 123*
- Desserts   *pages 124 - 134*
- Tequila Guide - Introduction, The Facts- Dispelling the Myths, How to Drink Tequila, Recipes - Margarita, Sangrita.   *pages 135 - 138*

The Story

TWO COOKS AND A SUITCASE

THE WEE RUBBER THING THAT FITS OVER THE END OF THE WALKING STICK TO STOP THE WOOD FROM CRACKING

The door of Lupe Pinto's Mexican/American Grocery Store in Tollcross, Edinburgh eased open and a frail looking old man with yellow fingers appeared in the doorway. Shuffling towards the counter he raised his stick to within inches of my nose.

"D'ye sell these Sonny?"
"What? Walking sticks?"
"Dinnae get smert wi' me Sonny.
Ah mean the wee rubber thing that fits o'er the end tae stap the wid fae crackin."

My partner Rhoda explained that the shop only sold groceries, so Nicotine Man shuffled back out the door while we considered renaming the shop to
"*Lupe Pinto's Mexican/American Grocery And Orthopaedic Supplies Store*".

TWO COOKS AND A SUITCASE

It did occur to me though that if this old guy had wandered up to a stall in Oaxaca's busy central market he might reasonably have expected to find what he was after among the chiles, fresh cheeses, hot sauces, tomatillos, annato seeds, washing machine spares, lubricating oil and who knows what else: *"The wee rubber thing that fits o'er the end tae stap the wid fae crackin? Sure, just reach behind that sack of garbanzo beans."* After all, Lupe Pinto's Deli was inspired by our experiences of Mexico and its markets.

So, in recognition of the strangest request we've had to date and for the sake of authenticity, we now stock the wee rubber thing, in grey only, for £2.50.

The following is the story behind Lupe Pinto's Deli and the recipes in this book. It's the story of two cooks, a suitcase, and a year long quest for great US and Mexican cooking.

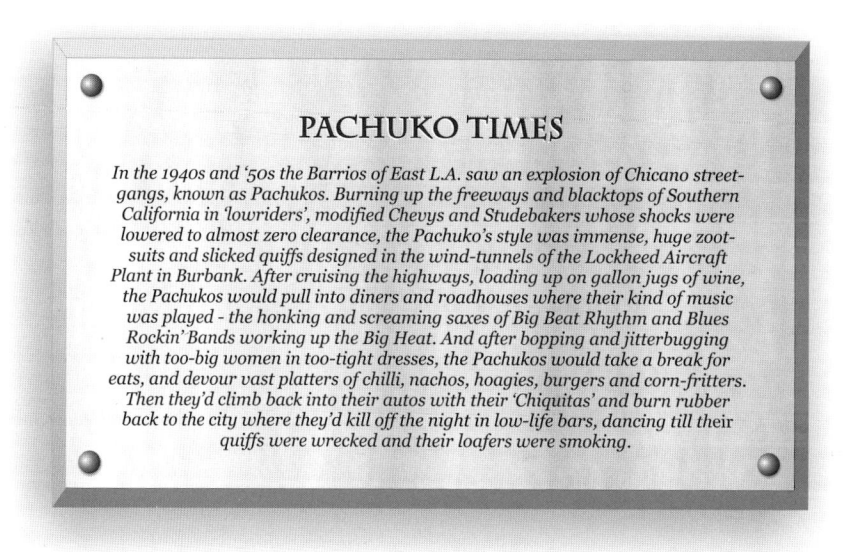

PACHUKO TIMES

In the 1940s and '50s the Barrios of East L.A. saw an explosion of Chicano street-gangs, known as Pachukos. Burning up the freeways and blacktops of Southern California in 'lowriders', modified Chevys and Studebakers whose shocks were lowered to almost zero clearance, the Pachuko's style was immense, huge zoot-suits and slicked quiffs designed in the wind-tunnels of the Lockheed Aircraft Plant in Burbank. After cruising the highways, loading up on gallon jugs of wine, the Pachukos would pull into diners and roadhouses where their kind of music was played - the honking and screaming saxes of Big Beat Rhythm and Blues Rockin' Bands working up the Big Heat. And after bopping and jitterbugging with too-big women in too-tight dresses, the Pachukos would take a break for eats, and devour vast platters of chilli, nachos, hoagies, burgers and corn-fritters. Then they'd climb back into their autos with their 'Chiquitas' and burn rubber back to the city where they'd kill off the night in low-life bars, dancing till their quiffs were wrecked and their loafers were smoking.

PACHUKO TIMES

Our restaurant, 'Pachuko Cantina' was a tribute to this life, the food that fuelled it and, especially, to the honkers, screamers, shouters and wailers that gave American R'n'B its backbeat.

Opening the restaurant one afternoon, I noticed a cuban-heeled, Rayban-wearing cool dude bobbing up and down excitedly as he read the Pachuko Times plaque on our window. I said *"Hello"* but he was already off, walking up the road, heels clicking.

That evening the dude - Ken Vallante by name - returned. We fed him and over after-hours drinks he pitched his dream of driving his 1961 white Cadillac across the US. We were inspired. We could travel with him, collecting recipes and getting the lowdown on real American food. Forget the hamburgers and hot dogs - what about Tex Mex, the fantastic food of the South with dishes like Shrimp Creole, Cajun Gumbo and Hush Puppies? What about Mexico with all its great regional dishes?

For the next twelve months the restaurant was bursting at the seams, fully booked every night, with a two-week waiting list for tables at weekends. We'd spent three years creating a rocking, fun restaurant. It was just what we'd set out to do, but we couldn't stop dreaming our American dream. Then, from nowhere, our chance appeared. A customer offered to buy us out. Within the month the place was sold, a fat cheque was waiting to be spent and we were ready to go.

The ground rules were:

- No backpacks - backpacks are for ramblers and we were the Travelling Cooks.
- Lots of hair gel for my quiff.
- We'd go for a year.
- We'd always make sure our pants were clean and fresh.

TWO HOURS LATE FOR KEN VALLANTE

Our arrival in Boston was delayed for two hours, which was bad news for most of our fellow passengers, but all it meant for us was free in-flight champagne.

Life seemed great until we hit immigration. Looking like the Tasmanian Devil in a uniform, the immigration official eyed my well-gelled quiff from her station. I was sixth in line in her queue and she hated me already! On discovering we had open-ended return tickets she became very suspicious. I explained that we were the Travelling Cooks and that we planned to make our way across America, savouring the delights of regional cuisine and then head for Mexico to do the same. She led us to her interrogation room for a forty-five minute session of baggage rifling and questioning.

> *"Why do you want to spend a year in America?"*
> *"Why do you have American friends?"*
> *"Do you plan to seek employment in America?"*

Although we had the relevant guide books for the US and Mexico and a letter from our bank, saying: *"Large spendable wad, available immediately for squandering on frivolous fun"*, it seemed nothing we said could persuade

TWO COOKS AND A SUITCASE

her of our innocence - until she discovered an entire layer of the suitcase composed of condoms.

"Do you plan to get much rest in the coming year?" she smirked. *"Pack your bags. Have a good trip."*

We were tired, our enthusiasm had waned, and the cheap champagne was wearing off. Then we saw her. The '61 big finned white Cadillac, with cuban-heeled, Rayban-wearing Ken Vallante leaning against it, arms folded.

"Welcome to America. What kept you? Need a ride?"

PLANET LEE

The day after we arrived Ken took us to a Woodstock revival party in an apartment block owned by a veteran hippy called Lee and before the night was out we'd struck a deal to rent our first Test Kitchen. It was perfect: low rent, a cooker, great local shops and it was lively at night too, what with drug dealers arguing, police sirens wailing, drunken brawls and the odd gunshot. A funky, good choice, we thought.

Our Landlord Lee turned out to be pretty funky too. On our introductory tour of the house, we relised that he had us down as a primitive Celts, used to a simple way of life, long since forgotton on American shores.

He explained to us that there are two types of washing machine in America - front loading and top loading - and that they use powder detergent. To spare our blushes he also assured us that mountain springs contain their own natural detergent and that cleaning your clothes in them is all right too. Naturally we didn't attempt to enlighten him.

We started knocking the place into shape straight away, borrowing all the cooking utensils we needed from a junk shop run by our neighbour and making a dinner table with old wood we found in the basement. After a few days Test Kitchen 1 was ready for action.

With guests due round to sample our first batch of new recipes, we discovered we were two plates and a saucepan short of a perfect dinner. Rhoda made me flip a coin and I lost. I climbed the stairs to Lee's apartment and knocked a couple of times. There was no answer, so I entered and there was Lee, dancing round a sculpture he was creating and wearing nothing but a pair of headphones. As he took them off I averted my eyes from his low-hung wang and asked if I could borrow some dishes and a cooking pot.

"Sure. Help yourself, Doug." As I scurried out with the stuff, he enthused: *"Sometimes I like to get naked and sculpt."*

CHITLINS

Just two blocks from our apartment was the neighbourhood favourite, Bob the Chef's Soulfood Restaurant. On our first visit the waitress, a huge black lady who sounded like the cook in Tom & Jerry, came to take our order. Ken never ate at Bob's without ordering the out-of-this-world ribs, while I asked for pork chops with black-eyed peas

and cornbread. Rhoda, though, decided to opt for something a little more unusual.
"Chitlins please."
"You eat Chitlins Honey?"
"Eh. Yeah, sure."

To be honest neither of us was sure. We'd heard the term in lots of blues songs, in the context of *"ain't got nothin to eat but chitlins"* and had assumed it was chicken wings or something but as the steaming pile of shredded corset arrived, we realised that Rhoda had made a dreadful mistake. The only way I can describe the taste of Chitlins (boiled pigs intestines) is to liken it to solidified bad breath. Thankfully, the rest of the food was delicious, with loads of cabbage in which to bury the inedible chitlins, creating the illusion that Rhoda did in fact eat them.

CADDI TRIPS

The plan to drive with Ken across the States in the Caddi fell through due to his work commitments, but we didn't let this stop us living out our American dream to the full. It was during our stay in Boston that we picked up the habit of taking side-trips from wherever we based ourselves. As well as food, these excursions tended to feature copious longneck and bourbon chaser sessions. Our best Boston side-trips belonged firmly in the rock n' roll category, with Ken at the wheel of the Caddi driving like a madman, puffing on Clove cigarettes, and Chuck Berry blasting out of the antiquated in-car sound system. To Ken these excursions were a taste of what might have been, to us they were an inspiration.

TRIP 1 - QUIFF-FLICKERS NIGHT AT SHITKICKERS BUNNY BAR

Route 1 used to be the main highway connecting Maine with Florida. Although it no longer exists in its entirety, sections of it survive as 'Highways of Fun', with huge restaurants boasting the biggest meal, the longest drink etc. The Caddi pulled into the parking lot of a sleazy Bunny Bar where a local radio station was holding a Quiff-Flickers night. *"Nice '61 man!"* a bull-necked rocker shouted from his groovy '50s Hot Rod. Ken winked over as we headed for the bar. Inside the clientele was a mixture of good ole rockers, there for the music, and fat guys with ill fitting slacks and dandruff, who I presumed were there for the pleasure of being served by tall shapely women dressed as rabbits.

The music was fantastic. Big Joe Turner's 'Shake, Rattle & Roll' hit the turntable and we hit the dance floor. Three minutes of quiff thrashing, spinning and leg trembling and we were through to the final of the jiving contest - a pleasure we would have to forego as hunger was setting in. The memory of Frank's neon, boasting 'America's Biggest Steak', drew us like a magnet out of the Bunny Bar, into the Caddi and back down Route 1.

We arrived to find a queue of about four hundred people. Waiting seemed out of the question, but Ken assured us this was no big deal at Frank's and, sure enough, we were seated within half an hour. The sheer size of Frank's is impressive - it has six dining rooms and ours alone held around two hundred people. The menu consists of steak, steak

TWO COOKS AND A SUITCASE

and more steak. I think there's a fish pie in there somewhere, but nobody goes to Frank's for fish pie.

We ordered salad starters with the 3/4lb filet mignon to follow. Portions in America are generally ridiculous, but Frank's has to take the Greedy Bastard of the Year Award. The salad starter alone must have weighed a couple of pounds, including the 8ozs of creamy ranch dressing and enough bread rolls for a family picnic. There must have been twenty cows worth of beef on the tables in our dining room. As they ate, people all around us were developing muscles they didn't even know they had. The guy at the neighbouring table doubled the girth of his neck in the time it took him to chomp his way through what looked like a 2lb T-bone.

The next day Rhoda and I got up and walked from Boston's south end, across the bridge into Cambridge and back again to the centre of Boston. We walked for eight hours, stopped only once for coffee, and ate nothing all day. Pure protein

TRIP 2 - PINK MEAT AND FRIED SURFBOARDS

Salisbury Beach Town, north of Boston, is testament to the fact that for every good American regional cuisine outlet there are at least 10 nasty food shacks. Huge wobbly parents accompany huge wobbly children from entertainment kiosks to fast food shacks. It's supposed to be fun, but disappointment comes fast. Trying to win a goldfish by throwing a dart at a target the size of a postage stamp is tough enough, but it's virtually impossible when your throwing arm weighs a bulbous 60lb or so. To compensate for the huge disappointment of losing, the kids waddle over to the nearest fried dough counter. Fried dough, which comes in portions the size of surfboards, is deep-fried in a large vat of oil and then coated in powdered sugar - Mmmh! As the sugar kicks in a short period of intense excitement ensues, usually leading to an attempt to win a huge inflatable hammer by performing yet another impossible feat. Then it's time to seek solace once more by guzzling a foot long neon pink hot dog. And so the cycle continues until at least one more chin appears.

Meanwhile, not fifteen minutes' drive away stands Brown's, one of the oldest and finest lobster shacks on the East Coast. There we could tuck into fresh lobster, home baked bread, coleslaw and corn on the cob, while back in Salisbury Beach the diabetic nightmare raged on.

THIRTY SIX HOURS ON A TRAIN

Our main food interest lay in the Soulfood, Creole and Cajun cooking of the South. As we settled into our seats for the first leg of the train journey to New Orleans, we reflected on some of the funky weirdos who'd turned up in the previous week looking to rent our apartment and wondered who Lee would choose to replace us:

1. The Russian music teacher - looking for pupils and a place to play his piano?
2. The young would-be pop star - looking for a cool pad and low rent?

3.   Two elderly Polish immigrants - no English spoken, looking for America?
Through thick glass we watched America slowly changing, and occasionally dozed off to awaken to a new vista. My excitement mounted with each passing hour. I had been dreaming of New Orleans for years and now the place I'd read so much about, the music I'd collected and listened to, the recipe books I'd studied, were less than a day away.

As night fell, the picture show outside drew to a close. We walked into the bar carriage to find a few like-minded folks already scoffing bourbon. Within an hour the bevvy carriage was full of people getting loaded and a bit of a party atmosphere was developing. A black girl with a beautiful singing voice made eyes at a young soldier as they skilfully ad-libbed, trading lines from soul ballads to say how much they adored each other. Others began to join in the singsong and then, as a soulful rendition of 'Amazing Grace' drew to a close, a fellow passenger piped up:
"Wait a minute. That's a Scottish song. You two are Scottish. Let's hear you sing a Scottish song." After a few chants of encouragement from the drunken crowd, we found ourselves arm-in-arm, singing away and soon everyone in the carriage was bellowing *"Donald where's yir troosers?"* at the top of their voices. The party rolled on late and I woke early, stinking of bourbon and with no recollection of returning to my seat, but still full of excitement.

We returned to the bar carriage for coffee and breakfast. Our companions of the previous evening had left the train earlier to be replaced by a new group. The barman was still there though and he offered us a bourbon on Amtrak. We declined, opting for Bloody Marys instead.

By the time the train reached Lake Pontchartrain the bright orange sun was sinking fast, illuminating the still water and silhouetting the twisted trees draped in Spanish moss. I half expected to see Tom Sawyer skipping across the banks eating a catfish supper. New Orleans was nearby and I was so excited I could hardly speak. When the train pulled in we took off out of the station into the thick humid New Orleans air.

Some dude was yelling *"Taxi folks! C'mon folks!"* People ignored him and joined the ever-growing queue. We asked him what the deal was. *"You give me a dollar and I'll have you packed into a taxi in twenty seconds."* One dollar and twenty seconds later we were heading for the French Quarter. Checked in, showered and dressed to impress, we sauntered up the quiet side street from our hotel into the mayhem of Bourbon Street, downed a couple of infamous Pat O'Brien's Hurricane Cocktails and headed to a Creole restaurant for Cajun Bar-B-Q Shrimp, Scallops Creole, Fried Cheese and Gumbo. Stuffed and tipsy, we were meandering back towards our king sized bed, when a junky shoe shine boy hit on us with his daft scam:

> *"I bet I know where you got dem shoes! If I know where you got dem shoes, I git to shine dem shoes."*
> Hassle, hassle, hassle.
> *"Okay, where dude?"*
> *"You got dem shoes on your feet, on the street in N'Orleans. Dat'll be $20 for the bet and $20 for the shine."*

We gave him $5. Much more than a shoe shine costs, but he looked menacing and we could see a gang of his fellow druggies congregating a few yards away. We dashed off to find a busier street and sought refuge by a parked cop car until we were sure no one had followed us.

TWO COOKS AND A SUITCASE

THE BIG EASY

The hotel was booked for three nights only - it was time to start looking for Test Kitchen 2. We called up Steve and Kelly, some friends of a friend in Boston. These two names and a phone number on a crumpled piece of paper turned out to be our passport to New Orleans. Normally the 'friends of a friend' situation results in a brief encounter and embarrassing silences, but on this occasion we struck gold. Steve and Kelly turned out to be a couple of like-minded hell-raisers and our hunt for accomodation was to turn into a drinking and eating binge in their company.

They picked us up at the hotel and took us to the Saturn Bar on the outskirts of the French Quarter. This crumbling bohemian art shack is an accidental work of genius: '50s games machines silent and stylish next to their flashy, techno sounding replacements; '40s radios beside the satellite T.V.; hand painted beer signs from a hundred years ago; multicoloured neons and bar paraphernalia from every era of the twentieth on the walls; and at the back, a dusty art gallery with great pictures hung badly.

We were shooting pool and downing Tequila when some of Steve's friends strolled in. Ryan, Marcus and Mark were on a boys' night out. By that, I don't mean eight pints and a vindaloo - these laddies were getting tanked up ready to cruise some camp strip joints. Many drinks and much banter later, we jumped into the back of the boys' pick-up and were dumped outside our hotel, totally steaming. The pick-up screeched off, with parting cries of *"No straights allowed where we're gawn! Bye. See y'all tomorrow"* and peals of hysterical, camp laughter.

We got up early, with only one day left to find accommodation. During the morning we scoured the French Quarter for a reasonable rent deal, but if such a thing exists we didn't find it. In the afternoon we rode the streetcar uptown to check out Ryan's kind offer of a room rental. He greeted us on the 'poach', covered from head to toe in dust and clutching a six pack of Dixie longnecks. He had warned us that he had only recently returned to New Orleans from California and that his semi-renovated house needed some urgent attention. Boy was he right! We chucked back the beer and he laid down the deal: *"Help me gut the house and decorate the back room and it's yours real cheap."* We shook on it. The search for Test Kitchen 2 was over almost before it had begun.

Despite its condition, the house on Spruce Street in the Carlton area is a fine example of New Orleans architecture. Stripped of paint to expose the natural cypress wood, it creaks and bends with the seasons. It is a raised double shotgun style building. That is, two rows of rooms running side by side with no connecting corridors, and a great big porch to sit on and swill beer.

Our room, at the end of one row and right beside the kitchen, overlooked a wild backyard with a pecan tree full of squirrels. The kitchen was a white tiled room with a Chamber 1965 gas range and all the utensils we needed. In the next-door barrel of the shotgun, lived Charley the Dog with Mississippi Cecil, an ex-preacher, who had taken to drink and photography following an encounter with the devil. Just ten seconds away was Jake's Corner Store, selling every part of the pig but the oink. The neighbourhood was full of good cooks and eating places, and the French Quarter was just thirty minutes away by streetcar.

One week and several crates of Dixie later, Test Kitchen 2 was fully operational and word soon got around that the Travelling Cooks were in the neighbourhood. We collected and test-cooked recipes from shopkeepers, cooks, neighbours, friends, anyone we could, and before long we were ready to host our first big banquet. We set a huge wooden table on the back porch and served up Stuffed Cabbage in Creole Sauce, Stuffed Mushrooms, Shrimp Curry, Cajun Potato Salad and Corn Bread for sixteen people. Dinner was rounded off with Mint Juleps and we sat into the wee small hours discussing how many eggs go in a Pecan Pie, who makes the best Cajun Hot Sauce and Chicken Fried Steak and how many dangleberries you can find on a bear's arse.

SOULFOOD SUNDAYS

Sundays are Soulfood days, when families traditionally gather to feast on comfort food, and for us there was no Soulfood experience to better Sister Alberta's.

Sister Alberta runs a restaurant from her home. There is no menu; she simply recites what she can cook using the day's groceries and whatever her husband John has bagged on fishing or hunting trips. The jukebox is full of old classics - Muddy Waters, Sam and Dave, Bessie Smith and, in the Gospel section, two songs by Sister Alberta herself. Signed photos of some of America's soul heroes hang above the jukebox. One of James Brown carries the handwritten message "You're the best". I couldn't be sure whether this referred to her cooking, singing, hospitality or to all three.

On the evening of our first visit, John was watching basketball on TV. As the game drew to a nail biting conclusion we tucked into Poke Chops 'n' Gravy, Fried Shrimp, and Soul Fried Chicken (dry and crisp on the outside, juicy and bursting with flavour on the inside). After home made Pound Cake and Custard, Sister Alberta sang and John told fishing stories, while we laughed and sang along till the Bourbon bottle was empty.

THE EUNICE SHUFFLE

"WELCOME TO EUNICE – Drive-through Liquor Shack 200 yards"

Any town boasting a drive-through liquor shack can't be all bad. We arrived at Kelly Keller's house just in time for evening supper - a bowl of piping hot Cajun Gumbo with Potato Salad. This particular Gumbo was wonderful, a dark rich roux full of pungent spices and piles of steaming hot Crawdad (crawfish) with Budin Sausage. After a couple of hours, rocking back and forth listening to the crickets and the distant sound of Cajun fiddlers, it was time to get our stomping gear on.
The grand Cajun Ball at the local community hall, with John Delafosse and the Eunice Boys heading the bill, was well into party overdrive when we arrived. There was no bar at this shindig, you brought your own and paid for ice and plastic cups at the door. Our party squeezed around a table and set about demolishing a few pints of 'Early Times'

TWO COOKS AND A SUITCASE

whiskey. This was a real community dance. Rowdy Cajun cowboys strutted their stuff on the dance floor, hoping to attract the attention of fine Southern belles; others grouped up to perform Cajun square dances; and trays of hot, spicy Jambalaya were passed around the hall.

The first pint of 'Early Times' was almost done when the band struck up the 'Eunice Shuffle' - same tune and moves as the 'Harlem Shuffle', but with a Zydeco backbeat - and we joined in one of the biggest sequence dances I've ever seen, all do-do-doing the Eunice Shuffle. I spotted an old black guy cocking his hat, popping his body, sliding his limbs and shuffling his feet to a level of cool only attainable through a lifetime's exposure to bluesy Afro-American sounds and dangerous corn liquor.

After the dance I went to speak to this hero but, despite his agile movements, he was too plastered to do more than grunt and give me a toothless grin. It was a different story with his friend who, on hearing my accent, asked in perfect Glaswegian:

> *"Hey pal where ye fae?"*

Turned out this black Creole cowboy had been brought up by a Scottish nanny and could turn the accent on at will. For the first time on our trip we were able to speak normally and be perfectly understood, by a Creole cowboy of all people.

THE ANGEL WITH A DEVIL BETWEEN ITS LEGS

"Tileman! Yes? No?" Ryan appeared at the door of our room, covered in grout and wearing a dress made of threaded bits of broken tile. *"Haven't you guys thought about your Halloween costumes yet? It's only a few days away!"* He disappeared and returned later wearing a red jump suit covered with splatterings of red and orange paint and a frizzy red permed wig festooned with party spray streamers: *"I'm thinking 'Fire', what do you think guys?"* In the coming days strange apparitions kept popping in to ask *"What do you think guys?"* Often it was clearly Ryan spray painted and wearing old clothes, but on one occasion an armchair with human legs appeared at the door and a muffled *" 'Upholstery Man!' No? Yes?"* came from deep within a pile of cushions. 'The Ghost of Steve's Hair', a white angelic apparition with huge wings and a mousy brown trimmed wig, made a short appearance and then transformed itself finally into 'The Angel With A Devil Between Its Legs'.

We donned a few left-over props and headed for the Bywater Decadence Day Ball. Held in a crumbling mansion house and gardens, this was a truly riotous affair featuring live bands, good food and naked mud wrestling. After a short side trip to an old-fashioned neighbourhood bar we returned to find the Angel With A Devil Between Its Legs rolling in the mud bath, squealing with laughter as he tried to fend off a mischievous lesbian dwarf.
The following evening was Halloween and we sat on the porch dishing out candy to the local kids, enjoying the array of spooky outfits. Later we headed for the nearby Carlton Bowling Alley to watch drunken ghouls dance and play bowls to the strains of the 'Swamp Monsters' rockabilly band.

The witch in Lane 8 gave it her best shot. As the 10 ball connected with the central pin there was a loud explosion and clouds of smoke billowed through the hall. The lights went out, the sound system shut down and we heard coughing and a few mystified utterances like "*Holy shit!*" "*What the fuck's goin' on?*" A soft humming began and a green light appeared from behind Lane 8. The hum grew louder, the light grew stronger and from behind clouds of thick smoke a large caped figure appeared. As the smoke cleared, the band struck up a wicked rockabilly rendition of 'You Ain't Nothin' But A Hound Dog'. The reincarnated Zombie Elvis danced stiff-limbed for a few numbers, then disappeared again at the back of the lane to rapturous applause.

This marked the end of Halloween at the Carlton Bowling Alley and indeed for everyone in New Orleans. Flamboyant costumes disappeared into basements all over the City. For 'The Angel With A Devil Between Its Legs' another frantic week was over. He returned to house restoration and we returned to researching, cooking and writing up recipes.

THANKSGIVING

Thanksgiving dinner was held at Cathy's house, two doors away. Cathy, herself an accomplished cook and enthusiastic contributor to our recipe hunt, had decided to tackle an old Paul Prudhomme recipe with some of her own ideas thrown in. She took a chicken and stuffed a wood pigeon right up its Yas, Yas, Yas. Then she rudely introduced the pigeon and stuffed chicken into a turkey and slow cooked the whole lot in a charcoal roaster. Cathy stayed up all night burning pecan shells on the charcoal to infuse the layered birds with a rich nutty flavour. The stock drained into a collecting pan below the roaster to form a rich, creamy, pecan flavoured gravy.

All the guests chipped in. There was Ambrosia Salad, Cornbread Dressing from the bird stock, Succotash, Cornbread Muffins, Pumpkin Soup and Pumpkin and Pecan Pie. Friends and neighbours popped in and out throughout the day, eating the goodies and leaving their own offerings.

Later, we joined the trashed party casualties in the back of Marcus' pick-up truck and headed for the French Quarter. The whole area was in major party mode and the time had come to get into the strictly non-family aspects of Thanksgiving.

As Marcus drove us round a selection of 'special bars', the phrase *"No straights allowed where we're gawn!"* echoed in my addled brain. In the leather bar I could contain my bursting bladder no longer. I headed for the toilet, trying to look as nonchalant as possible as a big leather clad clone rose from his table and followed me. In the few seconds it took him to open the toilet door behind me I managed to blast about four pints down the lavvy and stuff my vulnerable pecker back in my trousers. He tried to engage me in some polite banter
  "*Where you from? What do you think of New Orleans?*"

and the like. I made some excuse about getting a round in and slunk away nervously. I burst back into the bar in a hetero-panic looking for 'ma wumman', but all I could see was a bar full of very male looking gays. A paranoid vision of waking up in some unexplored part of the French Quarter, wrapped in sellotape with a hamster stuck up my tattered ringpiece came upon me and I charged out into the night air. Outside I was greeted with taunting laughter and endless quips about the fresh meat shortage in New Orleans.

From there I have vague memories of drunken high energy disco dancing, breakfast at the Humming Bird Grill, and one very vivid memory of a near-naked woman being led on a dog lead by a large leather-masked man who was sadistically whipping her and dropping hot candle wax on her bare back.

GREYHOUND MISERY

It was now late in December. I awoke to the sound of Marcus and Rhoda having breakfast on the porch - coffee, pancakes and the usual lashings of bitchy banter:

> "Margaret Thatcher Thighs"
> "Queenie. Old Face. Poofy Breeks".

This latter particularly aggravated Marcus as its meaning was shrouded in mystery and would torment him for the rest of the day.

They were also discussing plans for our grand leaving party that night. We had truly fallen in love with the Big Easy and it was hard to tear ourselves away, but we had to remember that we were the Travelling Cooks and although we'd been cooking diligently, the travelling part had been somewhat neglected for the past three months. To say goodbye we served up the biggest feast yet - Creole Meatballs, Creole Chicken, Okra and Tomato Salad, Potato Loaf, Dirty Rice, New Orleans Style Stuffed Potatoes, Duck, Sausage, Okra Gumbo and Flaming Bananas with Vanilla Ice Cream.

The greyhound bus for L.A. departed late the following evening. We climbed aboard for the 48 hour journey, holding back the tears, and I quickly came to wish that we had been stretchered aboard comatose and fitted with Bourbon drips to keep us that way. After 6 hours of sweaty discomfort we were transferred to another bus, this time with a functioning air conditioning system. Unfortunately this vehicle was already near full and there were only two separate seats available for us. Rhoda's new travelling companion took one look at Baloo the Bear slumbering next to the other empty seat and refused to move and let us sit together. I was forced to shoe-horn myself into the window seat next to the lard mountain. Hours later, when the bus pulled into the next rest stop, he was still sleeping. With a strength born of nicotine craving and a desperate urge to be reunited with Rhoda, I managed to separate myself forcibly from the blubber tomb. Outside, I chain-smoked and tried to come up with a plan to get us sitting together again. Our 15 minutes up, I escorted Rhoda to her seat and looked up the bus to see nothing had changed - one seat next to Baloo and lots of people avoiding eye contact. I tapped Rhoda's neighbour on the shoulder:

"Look, I really do have to sit with my girlfriend."

My voice was calm, but I had the steely eyes of a killer and Rhoda's hatchet face spelt danger too. He shifted and the last we saw of him was a few hours later in El Paso drenched down one side in second hand sweat and looking close to a nervous breakdown.

Although we were together again, the journey continued to be a nightmare. I needed a drink. Close to the Texas State boundary we pulled into a parking lot for a rest break.

As we got ready to head straight for the beckoning neon of the liquor store, the driver came on the tannoy to remind us all that it was an offence to consume alcohol on the bus. We bought two quarter bottles of whiskey and headed separately for the bogs. I sat in a cubicle in the gents, forcing down the whiskey and chain smoking. I was sporting a thirty-six hour growth and stank of someone else's sweat. I looked, felt and smelt like a bum and I wanted to spend the rest of my life in the toilet. Eventually, Rhoda managed to coax me out and back onto the bus.

The final leg of the journey was a miserable blur. I remember immigration officials boarding the bus and checking everyone's ID. One asked us a question and I was sure that Rhoda answered him in German. They escorted a Mexican guy off and we continued. In Arizona I watched the silhouettes of mountains against the dark blue sky and later we passed thousands of windmills in a flat landscape. As we crossed the State Line into California the bus pulled over and officials boarded to confiscate our fruit. I thought I had finally cracked, but Rhoda assured me that this was actually happening. I guzzled our last banana and handed over the skin. We finally reached L.A. and the comfort of a friend's house.

As I dozed off I muttered to myself

"What an amazing six months."

"Yeah Amazing".

At least Rhoda answered in English.

OAXACA, SUPERAGUA AND NEAR-DEAD DOGS

After Christmas in L.A. we flew to Oaxaca, capital city of the southern Mexican State of the same name and famous for its indigenous Indian population, culture and good food.

TWO COOKS AND A SUITCASE

We disembarked at Oaxaca's tiny airport, watched our suitcase being wheeled to the terminal building on a large handbarrow and caught a VW combi van to our hotel in the hills overlooking the beautiful Spanish colonial city. It was still only two in the afternoon and the empty hotel swimming pool beckoned in the bright sunshine - we were about to learn our first lesson in Mexican culture.

A crowd gathered on the hotel patio to watch and applaud as we took the plunge. To begin with, I thought my knob had popped out of my shorts, but I checked and it hadn't. Later, as I strolled through town in my vest with Rhoda, we kept hearing cries of *"Hé Macho!"*. This stopped as soon as I put on my jacket and it dawned on us that, while it felt to us like a balmy June afternoon, to the Oaxaceños this was a cold winter day. What a bunch of Mexican sissies, they wouldn't last five minutes where we come from. That evening we drank Tequila and watched the sun set over the picturesque old city from the balcony of our hotel room.

Finding Test Kitchen 3 was priority number one. We had to look no further than the nearest travel agent. We saw three places and decided on a luxury apartment on Arteaga Street with two bedrooms, a kitchen, a huge living room and a lovely garden patio, all for $100 a week. We were right in the heart of town, close to the main square (Zocalo) and the central market.

Our first weeks in Oaxaca were punctuated by a series of market disasters. The first came when we paid something like 100 times too much for a loaf of bread. The Indian woman we bought it from took the money, then laughed right in our faces, making sure that all her fellow stall holders realised there were a couple of real turkeys heading their way. Everyone started jeering and laughing at us. The taunts were largely uttered in incomprehensible Zapotec dialect, but I caught the gist when a Spanish speaking vendor offered me a single onion for 1,000 pesos. We were laughed out of the market.

Spanish grammar was initially a problem too. Whereas at home one will ask a shopkeeper *"have you any eggs?"* or whatever, in Mexico it is customary to enquire *"are there any eggs?"* The first (and only) time I asked for eggs the British way the stallholder bellowed with laughter and pointed at his crotch: *"Sure, I've got eggs. Two great big hairy ones!"*

We learned fast and quickly narrowed down the stalls to the ones with the best prices, the least flies and the friendliest attitude. There was the egg lady (no Spanish or English spoken), Juan the cheese man, Lizi the spice and chile lady, who put us onto the hand made tortilla lady, and so on. Before long we were bartering with the best of them and a trip to the market became an enjoyable outing, rather than an embarrassing ordeal.

Another place we enjoyed browsing in was the witchcraft shop, which offered scary concoctions like ground armadillo shell for enhanced sexual performance, spell casting powders, chicken claws and snake poultices.

A strong sense of the surreal pervaded Oaxaca. Take the 'Super Agua' man. Each morning he drove his truck through the streets, pumping the horn and calling his wares through a loud hailer mounted on the roof of his cab. Each time he uttered the words *"Super Agua"* he intoned them differently. It wasn't unusual to hear a very sexy

"Super mmmmm (sophisticated pause), *Suuuper Aguoooowa"*, followed by a brusque *"Superagua!"*, a quizzical, almost wheedling *"Super Agua??"*, then a thundering Chac the Raingod *"SUPER-AGUA!!"* I would run from the house, grab a huge bottle of purified water off the truck, replace it with the empty, pay at the driver's window and wait for him to broadcast a sincerely grateful *"Super Agua"* as he drove on his way.

Or there was the masked wrestler on a bicycle, promoting his next fight through a megaphone with a very fit looking chained bear running along behind. Or the two young boys, each struggling under the weight of a severed, dripping cow's head. And on every street corner the near dead dog, panting slowly, and peeping through crusty eyelids.

HONG KONG LOBERTO

We'd polished off a meal of Chile Rellenas and Tamale Oaxaceno (corn dough filled with chicken and chocolate sauce and wrapped in steamed banana leaves), washed down by a couple of tequilas. As the Zocalo closed down around midnight we headed for home.

At the corner of our street we heard the strains of a Mexican pop band, accompanied by a drunken party whooping and hollering. We followed the sound, knocked on a heavy wooden door and bingo!, an enthusiastic host ushered us in and closed the door behind us. We were handed colourful gourd bowls and presented with a huge vat of weird looking liquid. I scooped some up and knocked it back praying that it wasn't pulque (a fermented agave drink with the texture of a snotter milkshake). Mercifully it turned out to be an exotic tropical fruit punch. We'd stumbled on a wedding party, but this was no society wedding, as Rhoda noted:

> *"Looks like we've just missed the clothes swapping game."*

This was good news, because the poorer Mexicans know how to throw a brilliant party and they're always happy to share what little they have. Being, rather obviously, visitors, we were encouraged to take part in every aspect of the mayhem. Before long, and without needing too much encouragement, we were attacking Piñatas blindfolded, throwing rice, dodging fireworks and enthusiastically accepting the never-ending invitations to dance. Eventually we retreated towards the back of the room to adopt a lower profile. It was there that we met Loberto, a hairlipped Mexican muchacho. We conversed as best we could, encouraging him to write everything down since we found him hard to understand, and because he showered us with saliva whenever he spoke.

As the wedding party drew to a close, Loberto suggested we accompany him to a late night bar and, like rats to sewage, we followed him down dark picturesque side streets. We let him do the talking at the door and got in without paying the usual entrance fee. A round of drinks arrived, the proprietor and his henchman joined us at the table, and things began to go wrong. Bags of drugs were produced - peyote, cocaine, and marijuana. We turned them down, quipping that whisky was all we needed to get high. More drinks were served, but the proprietor definitely had the wrong idea about us. He presented us with a handwritten price list to illustrate the savings involved in purchasing by the kilo and multiples thereof - this guy wanted us to ship stuff and I don't mean a couple of puffs of grass for the amigos back home.

We tried to explain that the Travelling Cooks were here to discover the wonders of Southern Mexican cuisine and asked if he'd like to share any of his recipes with us. He stomped off in a rage, leaving his big amigo to guard the table.

Rhoda tried to defuse the situation with flattery, telling knucklehead what a kind, fair man his boss seemed to be. Meanwhile our guide passed me a note scribbled on a Salsa flyer, which I read and passed discreetly to Rhoda – *"I am a karate black belt. You must run."* The bar owner returned, looking menacing and presented us with a *"hospitality bill"* for $100. Scared shitless, I counted out the going rate for two rounds of drink, doubled it to $10, slapped the money on the table and told him I did not have the head of a donkey. Loberto jumped to his feet and lashed out, flooring the henchman as we hared for the door and pounded up the street. Next morning, over a breakfast of Huevos Rancheros - hot cakes and honey, and strong black coffee - we tried to make sense of the notes scribbled on assorted cigarette cartons and club flyers from the night before. We concluded that in future we'd try to avoid following hairlipped karate kids into sleazy late night bars.

ZOCALO BOYS

Oaxaca City boasts one of the most colourful zocalos in Mexico. Fantastic restaurants surround this central square, each with its own special dishes. The bandstand comes alive most evenings and people gather to promenade and gossip. Shoeshine stalls provide the focus for heated political discussions, with patrons clearly valuing the polishers' opinions as highly as their ability to put a shine on leather. Groups of unattached girls circle the zocalo one way while male suitors cruise round the other, jingling car keys and trying to make eye contact. Street vendors, offering a colourful array of helium filled balloon animals, hammocks and sweets, tout for business. You can even hire a band of wandering street minstrels to add some musical accompaniment.

Our favourites were the marimba men. A marimba band usually consists of half a dozen pissed campesinos with a huge wooden xylophone. You give them money and they knock shit out of the marimba machine with wooden clubs. For a truly satisfying marimba experience, payers and players should be equally smashed and when the music stops it is customary to stand the thirsty players a round of tequilas, thus ensuring they maintain the level of inebriation required to satisfy the next customer.

Occasionally we'd share a table with other travellers. This was generally good news for them, since we could provide an insiders' guide to the best restaurants and market stalls in town. For us it was a chance to show off, especially when waiters brought an array of Antojitos to the table and called us by name. Visitors often asked at what stage we began to feel the locals had accepted us. Looking back, I guess we really started to feel at home in Oaxaca once the 'zocalo boys' began to treat us with a certain level of respect.

The zocalo boys are a band of smartly dressed, English speaking young thrusters whose main aim is to con gringos into buying them drinks all evening, the lone female traveller being the prime target, as she represents a potential shag as well as free drinks. To these guys, the ultimate goal is to have a gringo buy you drinks all evening before you steal his woman for a night of passionate sex. A more sinister zocalo boy scam involves selling grass to unsuspecting gringos before turning them in to the police, then getting a cut of the bribe money needed to save their hippy asses from jail.

We were happy enough to have reached a stage where we knew them all by name and they knew not to approach us uninvited and without money to buy their own drinks.
On one occasion we spotted a group of them at a table in the bar next door, looking as obvious as warts on a witch's nose. They were clearly planning to stitch us up. A new zoke on the block strolled over to our table:

"Hi you guys, how you like Mexico? You like to drink Tequila?"

Rhoda responded to his opening gambit with her usual panache:

"Fuck off Carlos, we're no buyin' you drinks! And there's nae chance ae a shag either!"

LUPE PINTO (REINE DE CARIBE)

We packed our clothes, recipes and souvenirs in the suitcase, handed in the keys to the apartment and went to find a barber. After three months in Oaxaca Rhoda was delighted with her longer sun-bleached hair, but I was looking a bit bedraggled. No amount of hairspray and gel could prevent my normally highly maintained quiff from looking like a splattered bleached beaver. Every salon displayed photos of elegantly coiffed Italian-looking studs yet, in practice, they all seemed to offer a choice of only two styles for gents - the 'Mexican short bowl' or the 'Mexican long bowl'. Finally I chickened out and we boarded the bus for Villahermosa, hair intact and loaded with booze.

We were travelling first class, a pure delight in Mexico, especially compared with the restrictions Greyhound bus travellers suffer in the USA. Once you've paid for your ticket, anything goes. We sat and watched hammy Mexican soap operas on the onboard T.V., smoked, drank and occasionally visited the bog. Just like a quiet night in really, except that every so often we'd pull into a bustling rest stop where you can buy anything from a Tamale to a tarot reading.

We arrived in the Mexican oil boomtown of Villahermosa with 14 hours to kill. As we dragged the suitcase around, searching for the non-existent left-luggage window, Alexandro Fernandez III presented himself to us. All Mexican bus stations seem to have their own eccentric, self-appointed officials. Usually you have to be wary of them, but the bizarre figure in military garb, saluting and smiling before us, turned out to be a real gem. This chance encounter

TWO COOKS AND A SUITCASE

resulted in a resting place for our luggage, a list of personally recommended restaurants and directions to the zoo, the park, the Archaeological museum and his favourite place for a slap up drink. We tipped him and he saluted, clicked his heels and marched back to the bus station to resume his duties.

From Villahermosa we travelled overnight to Merida on the Yucatan peninsula. Merida is a truly beautiful city and, with its abundance of restaurants, is the ideal place to investigate Yucatecan food. However, with spring temperatures soaring, we decided to try finding a cooler beach side location for Test Kitchen 4 and headed for Progresso on the coast.
We took to the place straight away. The town centre is packed with bakers, fruit shops, tortillerias, restaurants, bars and whorehouses for sailors suffering critical sperm build up. There is also a small but well-stocked fish and produce market and outside town are miles of sandy beach, lined with assorted bars and restaurants. On the esplanade decaying mansions crumble into the sea, while others have been restored to their former glory and serve as holiday homes for wealthy Meridanos.

It was out-of-season and the beach area was virtually deserted. 'Se Renta' signs were displayed everywhere and we realised we'd stumbled on a renter's paradise. We strolled on the sand, stopping to paddle and watch pelicans dive before finding a suitable Palapa style beachside restaurant called Capitan Mariscos. We were treated to an assortment of fresh seafood (shrimp, crab, fried fish, squid cooked in its own ink) and tortillas, accompanied by refreshing Mexican lager. We chatted with the staff who confirmed that renting accommodation in Progresso was as easy as falling down. When asked how to go about finding a place, the waiter advised us to walk one street up and four blocks along, then start shouting *"Lupe Pinto! Lupe Pinto!*
Everyone knows Lupe Pinto, she'll get you a house."

We thought about it for a while. Were we about to go around shouting the Mexican equivalent of something like *"Crazy Whore!"* in the hope that someone would stop laughing at us long enough to rent us a house? The lunchtime beers gave us the courage we needed and we staggered up the sandy street, lustily shouting

"Lupe Pinto! Lupe Pinto! Crazy Whore! Lupe Pinto!"

A young man wearing tight flared trousers and a frilly shirt waved us over from the side door of a bar:

"Lupe Pinto? I'll take you to her."

Lupe Pinto turned out to be a striking Mayan-featured woman, in traditional costume. She supplements the family income by looking after holiday apartments during the off-season. We explained that we were looking for somewhere old, close to the beach and cheap to rent, and she sent us off with her daughter Nani to view the left-hand side of a converted manse, one street from the beach. The other half of the house was uninhabited, the large porch area was all ours and there was sufficient cooking equipment to get Test Kitchen 4 up and running.

This time we would be researching a completely new type of cuisine. Yucatecan cooking features strong Caribbean influences with regular appearances from Jamaican Allspice, red hot pickled onions and chopped boiled eggs and is usually accompanied by the wicked heat of the chile habanero. What's more, with all the seafood you could possibly want available from the Gulf of Mexico just a fag-flick away, making it work in Progreso was going to be as easy as falling out of bed.

Next day we moved our suitcase from Merida to Progreso and found the entire Pinto clan gathered on the porch to welcome us. We quickly came to feel like part of their family. Lupe and her husband Carlos gave our mission their full backing and the recipes came flowing in. Carlos had been a fisherman and had cooked with the best of them until he was blinded by illness as a young man. Their three daughters - Pit, Emma and Nani - also became close friends and drinking companions.

Most Saturday nights they joined us on the porch for pre-disco cocktails and food sampling. Later we would flag down a passing pick-up truck and head for Disco Fale - a steamy, hot beach disco six miles up the coast. Mondays and Thursdays were Merida days, spent picking up some of the more exotic ingredients from the market and snooping around restaurants in search of some of the Yucatan's favourite dishes - Stuffed Cheese, Poc Chuc, Panuchos, Lime Soup. Otherwise, we just hung around, swinging in our hammocks on the porch. The weeks flew by and we discovered a level of relaxation we'd never experienced before.

As Easter approached we sensed something big was about to happen. The Pintos were run off their feet cleaning houses. The local naval school practised marching up and down the street, makeshift snack shacks started appearing along the Main Boulevard and a parade of trucks and cars, some with a lion or a bear sitting on the bonnet, passed our house. But none of this prepared us for the tidal wave of Meridanos that suddenly washed into town for the holiday break. Probably around 75% of the houses in Progreso are holiday homes. These fill to bursting point and all the tacky holiday complexes come alive as the population explodes by an amazing 50 times. New discos spring up and Merida's beautiful young things pose on beach buggies and motor scooters, displaying their wealth, sipping on soft drinks, waving and whistling.

If you can't beat them, join them. We hosted porch parties for our friends every night, just to show the Meridanos that we locals knew how to live it up too. After 2 weeks of mayhem, the wave of revellers swept back to Merida and Progreso reverted to a ghost town. The bats returned to the deserted mansion next door, the family of wild dogs re-housed itself in the beach shack across the road, the Pintos relaxed after their long round of cleaning houses with hangovers and we returned to the stove and Bar-B-Q.

THE BRIEFCASE

The briefcase (our hand luggage) had become an essential part of our year's journey. Its main function was to house paperwork: napkin scribbles, recipes, notebooks and rantings. However, for side trips the documentation was consigned to a drawer, and replaced in the briefcase by enough pants to keep us confident and fresh in the Yucatan heat. The briefcase was ready to go, but we were skint. We lay on the beach wondering who was responsible for the

TWO COOKS AND A SUITCASE

missing $1500 that should have been couriered to us three weeks previously. A month's fun money lost with less than a month to go before our year-long Boston-Edinburgh ticket expired. Along the sand, we heard the sound of excited voices drawing closer. It was Pit, Emma and Nani - who was waving a package above her head - and all of them were jumping and shouting. The money had arrived. We set off on a frantic three-week Mayan ruin-hopping, recipe-collecting, tour of the Yucatan.

We arrived at Uxmal early, before the busloads of tourists. From the top of the huge Pyramid of the Dwarf Magician we witnessed the arrival of a spectacular weather system. The towering thunderheads rolled towards us and we scurried down the side of the Pyramid. Uxmal took on an eerie dark green light and the air was burning as we raced to shelter in the ancient nunnery. For half an hour Chac, the Rain God, gave it his all, but as the storm abated, snakes, birds and lizards emerged from their hiding places and flowers burst into life before our eyes. Steam began to rise from the jungle and we left the arriving crowds of tourists to sweat in the open-air sauna. We visited Valladolid, a town famous for its special smoked sausage and the spectacular ruins of Chichen Itza nearby.

The final stage of the Mayan Ruin extravaganza was Tulum where we had to spend a night at the hippy campgrounds. In contrast to the breathtaking locations, these places leave me scratching. You hand over your Pesos, usually about the same as you'd pay for a budget hotel room with air conditioning provided, and in return you get the key to a beach shack, a candle and barely enough bog paper to wipe a gnat's arse. You have to shit down a hole in the communal lavvy, shower on the beach, and the food usually smells as bad as the sweat stained hammocks you have to sleep in. We found ourselves at the bar with Eurotrash, immersed in the suitcase versus backpack debate.

> *"Backpacks are lightweight, the weight is evenly distributed round many of the muscles in the body, thus preventing strain. They are waterproof or can be made so with the use of a spray. They are the preferred means of carrying belongings among young, alternative travellers. You can carry them easily on and off buses and trains."* argued the smart-arse German budget travel writer.

Rhoda's riposte:

> *"Suitcases have wheels and you can fit them in the back of taxis."*

And so the argument continued until Rhoda decided that Smart Arse had re-arranged himself (down below) once too often.

> *"We don't argue with Baw Howkers. If you can't organise a pair of fresh pants you're no' a traveller and you shouldn't be writing a travel book."*

A week later and almost a year to the day since we'd left, we stood at the Edinburgh Airport taxi rank - I pictured our tie-dye wearing German friend standing at the Guatemalan border, drenched in sweat and wearing an enormous backpack. I looked at our suitcase and thought *"Two Cooks and a Backpack"*. **What a crap name for a cookbook.**

The Basics

INTRODUCTION TO THE RECIPES

In a world full of good cooks it doesn't take long to collect a bunch of recipes. Walk into a place like New Orleans French Market, ask if anyone knows how to make a pecan pie, and you end up with a full debate on the subject plus handfuls of recipes. Similarly, a Mexican Market produces a wealth of knowledge as well as an abundance of handpicked produce.

Restaurateurs were another good source of recipe information, and being ex-restaurant owners ourselves, helped. A few shared stories and drinks brought down barriers and made trade secrets more accessible. Collecting recipes was the fun part. Wading through piles of scribbled notes, test cooking, deciding what to keep and what to file took the best part of ten years.

What follows is the end result.
We hope you enjoy them.

Dougie Bell

Rhoda Robertson

TWO COOKS AND A SUITCASE

THE BASICS

THE CUISINES EXPLAINED

CAJUN/CREOLE - the Food of New Orleans and surrounding area. The origins being a combination of French and Spanish settlers, African slaves, local Choctaw Indians and generations of immigrants including Irish, German, Croatian, Sicilian to name but a few. The French influence on Cajun food comes from the Acadians, French settlers ejected from Nova Scotia and resettled in the Louisiana countryside and Bayous.

Creole is associated more with the affluence of the big city, however the two cuisines have become inseparable over time, both including versions of classics such as Gumbo, Jambalaya and Cornbread.

SOULFOOD - Afro-American cooking, kissin' Cousin to Cajun/Creole. The term was derived in the '60s to describe what African American cooks had been preparing in neighbourhood restaurants, family homes and at Church meetings throughout the history of the south.

MEXICAN - When the Spanish arrived in the mid 1500s the indigenous population cooked with beans, squash, tomatoes, chocolate, vanilla, chiles, corn, fish, seafood, game (including wild turkeys) and an abundance of fruit, especially the avocado.

The Spanish introduced domestic animals and their own Moor-influenced cooking. The combination of cuisines spread throughout Mexico with each region producing its own local twists and ingredients.

OAXACAN - Famous for dark chile sauces with nuts, seeds and spices, as well as hand patted corn tortillas, masa dishes like Tamales, and locally produced Chorizo sausage. Traditional Zapotec and Toltec Indian dishes provided a great influence on Oaxacan cooking.

YUCATAN - Best known for the Habanero Chile - the hottest in the world - usually found present in table condiments, especially the deadly Red Pickled Onions. Much use of citrus juice and bright red annato paste as meat and fish marinades. There is also a Caribbean influence in the form of Allspice used in many dishes. A lot of this cuisine originates from the indigenous Mayan population.

MAKING A ROUX

This is an essential part of **Cajun/Creole** cooking, used in sauces, soups and Gumbos. The theory is basically the same as making a traditional French Roux, which is stirring butter or oil with flour for the base of a sauce. However with Cajun/Creole Roux the cooking process is continued over a very low heat for 15-45 minutes, stirring constantly with a whisk until the desired colour is reached. This can be anything from a light peanut colour to that of dark chocolate.

Because of the length of time it takes to make a roux we recommend that you make a large batch and use it by the spoonful for recipes throughout this book.

ROUX

500ml vegetable oil
220g plain flour
1 medium onion (finely chopped)

Heat the oil in a heavy-bottomed pan, whisk in the flour, and reduce to a very low heat. Stir continuously using a whisk, scraping the bottom of the pan, to make sure the flour doesn't get a chance to burn. Remove from the heat when the desired colour is achieved and stir the onions into the mixture. The roux will thicken to a paste as you stir in the onions. When cool put into an airtight container. It will keep in the fridge for about two weeks

1. light roux   -   approximately 15 minutes.
2. medium roux   -   approximately 25 minutes.
3. dark roux   -   approximately 45 minutes.

MEXICAN TECHNIQUES

MEXICAN GARNISH - when presenting Mexican dishes, go mad. Radish flowers, shredded lettuce, chiles cut into flowers, pickled red onions, coriander leaves - use your imagination. Many dishes are presented using the colours of the Mexican Flag - red, green and white. Salsa, Guacamole and Crema, for example

Garnish Tips:
- Make several cuts down the length of a chile and open out into a flower.
- Cut the top off a radish, peel the skin in four sections down **almost** to the base, place in cold water and the radish will open into a flower.
- Hard-boiled eggs can be chopped very finely, mixed with chopped parsley to create a lovely colour contrast and sprinkled over dishes. They can also be sliced or made into flowers.
- Canned roasted red peppers make a delightful garnish simply cut into strips.
- Coriander is used either whole leaf or finely chopped.
- Olives stuffed with pimientos can be sliced. Whole black or green olives look great popped on a blob of sour cream.
- Crema - thick crème fraiche or sour cream dollops on top of a dish not only represents the white of the Mexican flag but also adds texture and contrast. It also cools the effect of hot chiles and chile sauces.
- Toasted nuts and seeds - sesame seeds, pumpkinseeds, toasted chopped pecans or walnuts can add colour contrast to dark chile sauces as well as a delicious crunchy texture.

USING CHILES

Chiles are used dried, fresh and pickled throughout Mexican food. The heat factor is measured in Scoville units. This is a chemical measure of the capsaicin – the active heat ingredient present within the chile. This varies from almost undetectable to unbearable. Each chile has its own distinctive flavour. By drying the chile the flavour completely changes character, as is the case of fresh tomato versus sun-dried tomato. If you consider the huge range of fresh chiles available, the variation on flavour by drying them, and combining 2 or 3 in one dish then you can get an idea of the range and complexity of flavours available to you when experimenting with them.

Preparing Chiles
1. Fresh chiles - especially the larger ones benefit from being roasted and peeled. Grilling or toasting on a dry pan is the best method. When the skin is well browned and blistered all over, wrap in tin foil or pop them in a plastic bag to sweat for 10 minutes. The skin can then be easily removed. The seeds are best removed also, as they contain most of the heat and can be slightly bitter.
2. Dry chiles - roast them first on a dry pan, cover with boiling water until they re-hydrate - one hour should do it - then cut open and remove seeds. Lay the chile flat on a board, flesh side up, take a knife and scrape the pulp from the skin. You can spoon this directly into the dish you are making or blend it with spices and herbs to form a Recado (chile seasoning paste). Small dry chiles can be dropped whole, without preparation, into dishes and removed before serving.
3. Pickled Chiles - rinse off excess vinegar or brine and use in salsas, salads and sauces. They are particularly useful when fresh chiles are out of season. Pickled Chiles are great for garnishing or as a table condiment.

ROASTING AND PREPARING VEGETABLES AND SPICES

Roasting Spices - cumin seeds are used a lot in our recipes. Just lightly roast in a dry pan before grinding.

Roasting Tomatoes - many of our Mexican recipes use fresh tomatoes instead of canned, but you can substitute passata or sieved canned tomatoes when fresh ones are firm and tasteless. For best results, take the required amount of fresh plump tomatoes and roast them under the grill or on a dry pan until skin is browned and blistered. Peel off the skin and push as much as possible of the tomato through a sieve into the sauce or stew.

Roasting Garlic - most Mexican recipes require the garlic to be roasted until brown. This can be done under the grill with, or using the same pan as, the tomatoes.

Recado - Mexican spice blends, usually involving chile pulp, garlic, spices and annato seeds. Examples are Recado de Achiote (p83) and Recado de Pollo Pibil (p93).

THE TORTILLA AND MASA HARINA GUIDE

Burrito, taco, enchilada, tamale, what's what? When is a taco not a taco? The problem is that in Mexico descriptions and names change from state to state and even from restaurant to restaurant. I once witnessed a finger snapping American exclaim to a not too concerned waiter in Oaxaca that he had ordered tacos, not a bowl of chicken stew with tortillas on the side. Oaxacans roll their own tacos. Americans have categorised Mexican food whereas Mexicans are unconcerned about the massive variations.

Hopefully this guide will be useful but don't go waving it in the face of Mexican waiters.

BURRITO	A large wheat tortilla wrapped around a filling of your choice.
CHIMICHANGA	A deep or shallow fried burrito.
ENCHILADA	A small corn or wheat tortilla folded or rolled around a filling, topped with a sauce and finished with either crumbled or melted cheese.
ENCHILADA SUIZAS	'Swiss enchiladas'. A small tortilla rolled, smothered in sauce then baked or grilled with a good melting cheese.
STACKED ENCHILADA	Unrolled tortillas presented in a stack with filling and topping between each layer.
ENCHILADA PIE Or TORTILLA BAKE	Like a lasagne with tortillas replacing the layers of pasta.
TACOS	Corn tortillas rolled around a filling. Can be shallow fried until crisp, may come in the form of a pile of tortillas and a bowl of filling to roll your own.
TACO SHELLS	U-shaped corn tortillas fried crisp. An American fast food invention.
TOSTADA	Corn tortilla fried crisp, then topped.
QUESADILLA	Small uncooked tortillas folded over with cheese in the middle, pinched at the sides to seal in the cheese then shallow fried to produce small pasties. Variations include flour tortillas folded over cheese then pressed onto a hot dry cooking surface.
EMPANADA	As above with any filling other than cheese. Dessert fillings are very popular.
PANUCHO	Stuffed tortilla fried then topped with a filling of your choice.
CHALUPAS, SOPES	Tortilla dough shaped into a basket or boat then fried to form a receptacle for a huge variety of fillings and toppings.
GORDITA	A small flat tortilla patty, usually with another vegetable ingredient within the dough, fried or baked, then topped.

CHILAQUILES	Corn tortillas cut into strips then fried crisp. A soupy stew is then poured over them and various garnishes and toppings are added.
FLAUTAS	A rolled flour or corn tortilla usually shallow fried, it is flute shaped.

Tortillas - when unspecified, corn or wheat can be used.

HOME MADE CORN TORTILLAS

500g Masa Harina
600ml warm water

Mix the ingredients together with your hands to form a dough that is easily shaped without falling apart and not mushy. Knead the dough for 10 minutes, set aside for 30 minutes. Form the dough into small balls - the size of the ball defines the size of tortilla. Golf ball size will give you a 6-8" tortilla, although you may desire varying thickness.

Place a tortilla ball between two plastic bags and flatten it by:

1. using a traditional wooden tortilla press (very hard to find)
   or
2. pressing between two thick chopping boards. push down on the top one, or stand on it if you want thin tortillas.

Carefully peel the top bag off the tortilla, flip onto your hand and slowly peel off the other bag. Place on a hot griddle and cook for about 5 seconds on each side.

PACHUKO CANTINA
1940's - 50's
Mexican - Californian
Restaurant
3 GROVE STREET
EDINBURGH
Tel. (031) 228 1345
PROPS. D. BELL & R. ROBERTSON

TWO COOKS AND A SUITCASE

WHEAT TORTILLAS

800g plain flour
half tsp. salt
100ml luke-warm water
100g vegetable shortening

Rub the flour, salt and shortening together to form a mixture resembling fine breadcrumbs. Slowly add the water, mixing and kneading to form dough, cover and let stand for 20 minutes. Separate the dough into equal size balls the size of which depends on the desired size of tortilla. Roll out on a flat, floured surface. Cook on a medium hot griddle until the tortillas start puffing, about 1 minute.

If you can get good quality corn or flour tortillas you can save yourself a bit of work but be very wary of poor imitations.

TAMALES

IF YOU ONLY MAKE ONE RECIPE FROM THIS BOOK, MAKE TAMALES OR TAMALE PIE.

Tamale Dough
200g Masa Harina
100g butter or vegetarian shortening (melted)
250ml chicken stock
half tsp. baking powder
salt and pepper
filling of your choice (see below)

Sift the Masa Harina and baking powder, add the melted fat, stir in the chicken stock, and season. Stir well to form dough the consistency of cake batter, spread the dough over cornhusks, banana leaves or tin foil. You can make your tamales any size. If using cornhusks or banana leaves, simply trim down to desired size and soak in warm water for 15 minutes before spreading with dough. If using tin foil just cut pieces to desired size.
Add a filling (see below) and sauce, fold into little parcels seal with string and place in a steamer for 45 minutes.

LITTLE BUDDIE'S TINFOIL TAMALES, EEK!

Getting hold of corn husks or banana leaves can sometimes be difficult and can put people off making tamales. The use of either looks great and has the advantage of breathing steam into the tamale. To all tamale purists out there, here is a special message from Little Buddie Medina and myself.

"Tinfoil tamales are better than no tamales"

A little baking powder in the dough will lighten up the tamale, compensating for the lack of porosity of the tinfoil. The advantages include not having to soak leaves or fiddle with string, making tamales a little less daunting.

TAMALE PIE

Another easy option is to grease the inside surfaces of a casserole dish and spread the tamale dough over all sides and bottom. Add whatever fillings or sauces you have decided upon, spread a layer of dough over the top of the filling, seal with a lid or sheet of tinfoil and bake for 45 minutes.

For examples of this see: Yucatan Fish Pie on p65
   or   Chicken Tamale Pie on p99.

Ideal filling recipes
Suitable for any masa, tortilla or tamale dish
- Carnitas De Pollo *p35*
- Carnitas *p81*
- Refried Beans *p114*
- Chile Con Carne *p82*
- Pollo En Nogadas *p92*
- Picadillo *p78*

TWO COOKS AND A SUITCASE

BASIC RECIPES
USED IN MORE THAN ONE RECIPE

STOCKS

- Chicken Stock — page 35
- Creole Meat Stock — page 36
- Fish Stock — page 36

SAUCES AND CONDIMENTS

- Creole Sauce — page 37
- Mushroom And Peanut Sauce — page 37
- Tomato Sauce — page 38
- Chiltomate (Yucatan table salsa) — page 38
- Guacamole — page 39
- Salsa Fresca — page 39
- Salsa Verde — page 40
- Salsa Chipotle — page 40
- Yucatan Pickled Onions — page 41

CHICKEN STOCK
CALDO DE POLLO
Essential for recipes throughout this book.

1 large chicken (remove the breasts for another recipe or poach separately for 15 minutes)
1 carrot (roughly chopped)
1 large onion (roughly chopped)
1 tsp. Mexican oregano (substitute some sprigs of thyme for Cajun Chicken Stock)
1 stalk celery (roughly chopped)
4-6 cloves garlic
3 bay leaves
salt & pepper to taste
2 litres water

Place all ingredients in a large pot and cover with water. Bring to the boil, cover, reduce heat and simmer for 1 & a half hours. Once cooked, allow the chicken to cool in the stock. It will cool quicker if you turn the chicken now and again and stir the liquid. When cool, remove chicken, strain the stock and refrigerate. Remove the layer of fat that forms on the stock. Then freeze stock in small tubs for use in recipes throughout this book.

Makes 1 litre stock.

SHREDDED FRIED CHICKEN
CARNITAS DE POLLO
Shredded, fried crisp or bound together with cream cheese, this basic recipe makes a great topping or filling for many Mexican dishes.

*Use the chicken from **Caldo De Pollo** – remove all the meat from the bone and shred.*

6 spring onions (chopped)
4 cloves garlic
50g butter
200g cream cheese or sour cream
2 chopped chiles (Serranos, Jalapenos or Chipotles)

Melt the butter in a large non-stick frying pan, add garlic, onions and chiles. Cook for 2-3 minutes and then add the chicken. Keep turning until the chicken is well browned, if it gets a little dry add some stock. When ready, bind together with sour cream or cream cheese and use to fill tortillas. Alternatively skip the binding and sprinkle over Chilaquiles (see p97) or use in a salad.

CREOLE BEEF STOCK

a large beef bone
(roasted in the oven for 30 minutes)
250g smoked ham ribs
1 large carrot
1 stalk of celery
2 cloves garlic
1 medium onion
2 tomatoes (chopped)
2 bay leaves
1 sprig thyme
salt & pepper to taste
2 litres water

Place all the ingredients in a large soup pot bring to the boil, cover and simmer for 1 & a half hours. Strain the stock and cool. Remove the layer of fat from surface and strain again. Reserve the stock. You can freeze this in tubs for use in recipes throughout this book.

Makes 1 litre stock.

FISH STOCK

500g fish bones
2 stalks celery (chopped)
1 medium onion (chopped)
2 bay leafs
2 sprigs thyme
1 glass white wine
salt and pepper to taste
1.5 litres water

Place all ingredients in a stock pan, bring to the boil, cover and simmer for 30 minutes. Strain the stock and freeze in small pots until required.

Makes 1 litre stock

CREOLE SAUCE

Traditionally the bacon flavour comes from Tasso - a Cajun, smoked Pancetta

oil for frying
4 sticks celery (chopped)
1-bunch spring onions (chopped)
2 green peppers (chopped)
500ml chicken stock see p35
6 cloves garlic (minced)
50g of medium roux see p27
450g tin chopped tomatoes

720ml basil flavoured passata
or 720ml passata & 4 leaves fresh basil
4 sprigs each fresh thyme and oregano
1 glass red wine
150g chopped smoked bacon
or Pancetta *or* Tasso
100g of sliced mushrooms
salt and pepper to taste

Sauté the vegetables until soft (approx. 5min.), stir in the roux and slowly add the chicken stock. This forms the base to the sauce. Add passata, tomatoes, herbs and wine. Simmer the sauce on a low heat for 30 minutes, stirring occasionally. Meanwhile, fry the bacon until crisp, add the mushrooms, brown slightly and add this mix to the simmering sauce. Season and simmer for a further 10 minutes.

Makes one batch of sauce that can be frozen and used in recipes throughout this book.

MUSHROOM AND PEANUT SAUCE

50g butter
2 shallots (chopped)
1 small green pepper (chopped)
100g chopped mushrooms (sliced)
2 tbsp. medium roux (see p27)
200ml milk
50ml chicken stock
1 tbsp. peanut butter
Salt and pepper to taste

Sauté shallots and green pepper in the butter for 5-10 minutes until soft. Add mushrooms and cook for a further 2 minutes, then stir in the roux, coating the vegetables. Slowly add milk, stirring constantly to form a thick sauce. Stir in the chicken stock to thin the sauce. Add the peanut butter and simmer for 5-10 minutes to reduce slightly. Season with salt and pepper.

Makes one batch of sauce for use in recipes throughout this book.

TOMATO SAUCE

2 tbsp. oil for frying
1 medium onion (chopped)
2 cloves garlic
*250ml stock, chicken **or** beef (see p35 or 36)*
1 tsp brown sugar
*6 large tomatoes (roughly chopped) **or** 1 tin crushed tomatoes*
qtr. tsp. allspice (pimento)
4 leaves fresh basil
salt and pepper to taste

Heat the oil and sauté onion and garlic until soft. Add stock, sugar, tomatoes, allspice and basil. Simmer for 25 minutes. Blend in a food processor. Season with salt and pepper.

Makes one batch of sauce for use with recipes throughout this book.

CHILTOMATE MAYAN SAUCE

4 cloves garlic (minced)
2 medium onions (chopped)
6 tomatoes (roasted and strained through a sieve see p29)
*4 fresh epazote leaves **or** 1tsp. dried epazote*
1 Chile Habanero
250ml chicken stock
salt and pepper to taste

Sauté the onions and garlic until soft, add the sieved tomatoes, stock, Habanero and seasoning. Simmer for 20 minutes to allow the flavours to blend.
A very basic Mayan tomato sauce.

Makes one batch for recipes throughout this book.

GUACAMOLE

The availability of good avocados is essential for guacamole. The avocado must be ripe, the flesh must have a rich green rim, fading to pale green and then to yellow around the stone and have a buttery texture. You can check the ripeness by gently squeezing the neck of the avocado for softness. The best variety tends to be 'Hass' but if you can get the dull skinned variety with a red hue and dark skin, perfect. Avoid avocados with a shiny skin, as the flesh is usually very pale and the texture watery. Never use hard avocados. It is impossible to make good guacamole with these.

2-3 ripe avocados
(cut in half, remove stone and scoop out flesh)
2 tomatoes (roasted and peeled)
1 small onion
half a clove garlic some fresh coriander

1 Chile Jalapeno
juice of half a lime
half tsp. cumin seeds
(roasted and ground)
salt and pepper to taste

In a food processor mince the onion, garlic, tomatoes and Chile Jalapeno. Add the remaining ingredients and blend until desired consistency. Serve immediately or cover with cling film and refrigerate. If not serving immediately, save the stones and place them in the guacamole until ready to serve. This will prevent it from going dark.

SALSA FRESCA

1 kg fresh tomatoes (roasted and peeled)
1 clove garlic (roasted)
2 medium onions
1 small green pepper
1 small red pepper

some fresh coriander leaves
1 tsp. cumin seeds (toasted and ground)
some sliced Jalapenos (to taste)
juice of half a lime
half pint tomato juice (optional)

Prepare the tomatoes. Toast the garlic and cumin seeds, then crush the cumin. Place the tomatoes, garlic, onions, peppers and coriander in a food processor and chop. Add the ground cumin seeds, Jalapenos to desired strength, salt and pepper. If you would like a more liquid consistency, add tomato juice and blend.

SALSA VERDE

2 tblsps. oil
250g fresh tomatillos (roasted and crushed) or substitute canned tomatillos
1 onion (chopped)
2 cloves garlic
250ml chicken stock
a handful of spinach leaves
fresh coriander
3 fresh Chile Serrano
salt and pepper

Heat the oil and sauté onion and garlic until soft. Add tomatillos and chicken stock, and simmer for 5 minutes. Add the remaining ingredients and simmer for 20 minutes. Blend the sauce in a food processor or with a hand blender.

Makes one batch for use in recipes throughout this book.

SALSA CHIPOTLE

2 medium onions (chopped)
2 cloves garlic (chopped)
450g tin of tomatoes
2 Chile Chipotle (chopped)
1 tsp. cumin seeds (roasted and ground)
25g peanut butter

Fry the onions and garlic until soft. Add tomatoes and simmer for 10 minutes. Add Chile Chipotles, ground cumin and peanut butter. Stir until peanut butter is dissolved. Add salt and pepper to taste. Serve cold with a blob of sour cream or use as a sauce for cooking.

To convert the above salsas to cooking sauces for use with tortilla dishes, just add some chicken stock and blend the sauce to a smoother consistency.

YUCATAN RED PICKLED ONIONS

4 red onions (sliced thinly)
250ml red wine vinegar
2 cups boiling water
2 Chile Habanero fresh, dried or pickled (see p28 -29) (chopped)
half tsp. cumin
1 tsp. Mexican oregano
some epazote leaves dried or fresh
6 allspice berries
salt and pepper to taste
2 tbsp. red wine Vinegar
juice of half a grapefruit
juice of 1 lime
juice of half an orange

Pour all the ingredients except the fruit juices over the onions, mix well and soak for 4 hours. Drain the onions and place in a bowl with a little more vinegar and the fruit juices.

This is a very popular table condiment, served as an accompaniment to many Mexican Dishes.

Soups

- Peanut Soup — *page 43*
- Shrimp Bisque — *page 43*
- Zucchini Soup with Pecan Nuts — *page 44*
- Creole Tomato Soup — *page 44*
- Soulfried Chicken Gumbo — *page 45*
- Mr Keller's Seafood Gumbo — *page 46*
- Black Bean Soup (Sopa de Frijoles Negro) — *page 47*
- Cream of Avocado Soup (Sopa de Pollo y Aguacate) — *page 47*
- Lime Soup (Sopa de Lima) — *page 48*
- Seafood and White Bean Soup (Sopa de Puerto Angel) — *page 48*
- Chickpea and Chorizo Soup (Sopa de Garbanzo) — *page 49*

PEANUT SOUP

125g butter
4 spring onions (chopped)
1 stalk celery (chopped)
1 small green pepper (chopped)
500ml chicken stock or fish stock
100g smooth American peanut butter
salt and pepper to taste
150ml single cream
200g prawns (defrosted and drained) optional but highly recommended
chopped parsley

Melt the butter in a pan, sauté the onion, celery and green pepper until soft, about 5 minutes. Add chicken stock, stir in peanut butter, season with salt, pepper and Louisiana Hot Sauce. If you're adding prawns just simmer for less than 1 minute at this stage. Then stir in the cream. Serve garnished with parsley.
Serves 4-6

SHRIMP BISQUE

500g shrimp or prawns
(peeled, cleaned and chopped)
25g butter
1 stalk celery (finely chopped)
150g mushrooms (finely chopped)
1 spring onion (finely chopped)
25g grated carrot
1 bay leaf
pinch each of marjoram and nutmeg

salt and pepper to taste
juice from half a lemon
450ml chicken stock (see p35)
100ml single cream
1 heaped tsp. cornflour
6 cups cooked rice (see p120)
chopped parsley
sliced lemon

Melt the butter in a pan, sauté the vegetables for 5 minutes then add the chicken stock, lemon juice and seasonings. Cover and simmer for 20 minutes. Dissolve the cornflour in a little water and stir into the soup to thicken. Add chopped shrimp and cook for a minute. Slowly stir in the cream, make sure the pan is over a very low heat. Do not boil, as the cream will curdle. Ready to serve.
Put a cup of cooked rice in each bowl and ladle the soup over. Garnish with a slice of lemon and chopped parsley.
Serves 4-6

ZUCCHINI SOUP WITH PECAN NUTS

oil for frying
2 medium onions
2 cloves garlic
1kg zucchini (courgettes) chopped
500ml chicken stock

pinch of cayenne pepper
salt and pepper to taste
150ml single cream
150g pecans (chopped)
50g butter
chopped parsley

Sauté the onion and garlic in oil until soft. Add the chicken stock, chopped zucchini and seasoning and simmer until zucchini is tender. Purée the soup, return to a gentle heat. Lightly fry the chopped pecans in butter until they start to brown, remove from heat. Slowly, add the cream to the simmering soup. Do not boil. Serve the soup in bowls, sprinkled with pecans and chopped parsley.

Serves 4-6

CREOLE TOMATO SOUP

oil for frying
2 green peppers (chopped)
2 spring onions (chopped)
25g plain flour
500ml Creole beef stock (see p36)
10 medium tomatoes
(roasted and sieved) (see p29)

dash of Worcester Sauce
dash of Louisiana Hot Sauce
salt and pepper to taste
100ml single cream
150g mushrooms (thinly sliced)
25g butter
chopped parsley for garnish

Sauté the green peppers and spring onions in a little oil until soft. Add the flour and stir into the vegetables. Pour in the beef stock a little at a time, stirring constantly. Stir in the tomatoes, Worcester Sauce and Hot Sauce. Simmer for 30 minutes to reduce.

Meanwhile, for the garnish, sauté mushrooms in butter until softened. Drizzle a little cream on each bowl of soup, place on a few sliced mushrooms and some chopped parsley. Serve and enjoy.

Serves 4-6

Soups

SOULFRIED CHICKEN GUMBO
WITH CHORIZO SAUSAGE

a 1.5kg to 2kg chicken
1 tsp. each onion salt, cayenne pepper and mustard powder
300g flour
oil for shallow frying
500ml chicken stock (see p35)
1 green pepper (chopped)
2 stalks celery (chopped)
4 spring onions (chopped)
4 cloves garlic (chopped)
4 Chorizo sausages (chopped into bite size pieces)
400g tomatoes fresh or tinned (chopped)
salt and pepper to taste
half tsp. cayenne pepper
1 tsp. dried thyme
4 bay leaves
250g okra (topped, tailed and chopped)
chopped parsley
hot sauce of your choice

Batch fry the chicken (see Soulfried Chicken recipe p88). Once cooked set the chicken aside. Drain the oil, leaving the crispy bits in the pan and about 50mls of the oil. Over a very low heat gradually stir in 100g of flour, stirring constantly. Keep stirring for 15 minutes to form a roux. When the roux is cooked slowly stir in the chicken stock. This will form the base for your Gumbo. Leave this simmering on a low heat.

Sauté the vegetables, in a little oil, for 5 minutes until soft. Add the Chorizo and sauté for a further 10 minutes, then throw the cooked vegetables and sausage into the simmering Gumbo base. Add the tomatoes and all the seasonings. Simmer for 20 minutes then add the chopped okra and Fried Chicken pieces. Simmer for a further 15 minutes. In the last 5 minutes of cooking add chopped parsley and hot sauce.

Serves 8 as a starter or 4 as a main dish. Serve over rice or potato salad.

MR KELLER'S SEAFOOD GUMBO

oil for frying
2 tblsps. dark roux (see p27)
4 spring onions (chopped)
4 cloves garlic (chopped)
2 stalks celery (chopped)
1 green pepper (chopped)
1 red pepper (chopped)
500ml fish stock (see p36)
salt and pepper to taste
half tsp. cayenne pepper
2 bay leaves
half tsp. dried oregano
half tsp. dried thyme
100g okra (chopped)
400g crabmeat
500g peeled shrimp
4 hard-boiled eggs (quartered)
potato salad (see p104)
fresh parsley (chopped)

Sauté all the chopped vegetables, except the okra, in a little oil. Add the roux and blend with the vegetables. Slowly stir in the fish stock. Add all the seasonings and the chopped okra and simmer for 15 minutes. Add the crabmeat and shrimp, cook for just a few minutes.

The next stage is what makes Mr Keller's Gumbo. In a shallow bowl, spoon in a blob of potato salad, ladle over a portion of Gumbo, add some boiled egg quarters (2 per serving), and sprinkle with chopped parsley. Potato salad slowly dissolves in the Seafood Gumbo.
Not a bad idea Mr Keller.

Serves 8

BLACK BEAN SOUP
SOPA DE FRIJOLES NEGRO

500g dried black beans
500g ham hock or smoked ribs
sprig of epazote
50g butter
2 medium onions
4 cloves garlic

2 tomatoes (roasted and sieved)
2 Chipotle chiles (optional)
4 spring onions (chopped)
sour cream
pinch of pimenton (Spanish paprika)

Soak the beans overnight and then wash thoroughly. Place beans and ham hock in a large soup pot cover with water. Bring to the boil, reduce heat and simmer for 1 hour. Add boiled water to the beans as necessary. After cooking for ° an hour add the epazote. Meanwhile sauté the onions and garlic in butter until soft, add tomatoes and Chile Chipotle. Once the beans are cooked remove the ham hock or ribs, add the vegetables and simmer for 25 minutes. You can serve Black Bean Soup as a whole bean soup, though I prefer to purée the beans.

Serve in soup bowls with a blob of sour cream and sprinkled with chopped spring onions. A pinch of red paprika finishes the presentation. Some Mexicans sprinkle a little sugar on top. Mad Bastards! **Serves 4-6**

CREAM OF AVOCADO SOUP
SOPA DE POLLO Y AGUACATE

2 chicken breasts (rubbed with butter)
6 rashers bacon
2 avocados
500ml chicken stock (see p35)
2 tomatoes (roasted and sieved)
2 cloves garlic (roasted and minced)
2 Chiles Serrano (chopped)

small handful of chopped coriander
salt and pepper to taste
100ml single cream
100g freshly shelled peas
2 hard-boiled eggs (finely chopped)
1 pimiento (sliced into strips)
some whole coriander leaves

First grill the chicken until golden brown and bacon until crisp, then cut both into small pieces. Simmer the chicken stock on a low heat and add the sieved tomatoes, garlic, avocados, chiles, chopped coriander, salt and pepper. Simmer for 15 minutes. Purée the soup, add the shelled peas and cook for a further 5 minutes until peas are tender. Slowly stir in the cream.

Serve this cream of avocado soup with a handful of chopped chicken and bacon in each bowl. Garnish with chopped boiled egg, strips of pimento and some coriander leaf. **Serves 4-6**

LIME SOUP
SOPA DE LIMA

2 chicken breasts
1 red pepper (roasted, peeled and chopped)
or use a tinned pepper
1 Chile Jalapeno (chopped)
2 cloves garlic (minced)
3 medium tomatoes
(roasted, peeled and chopped)
1 medium onion (chopped)
juice of 2 limes
500ml chicken stock
salt and pepper to taste
6 corn tortillas cut into strips and fried crisp
100g chicken livers chopped fine and fried (optional)
handful of chopped coriander
a lime (sliced)

Place chicken, red pepper, Chile Jalapeno, garlic, tomatoes, onion, lime juice and chicken stock in a large pot, bring to the boil and simmer for 15-20 minutes. Remove the chicken breast, shred the meat and put to one side. Strain the stock to produce a refreshing consommé. Season to taste.

To serve, place some shredded chicken, crispy fried tortilla strips and a sprinkling of finely chopped chicken livers in a bowl. Ladle over the consommé, and garnish with a slice of lime and fresh coriander.

Serves 4-6

SEAFOOD AND WHITE BEAN SOUP
SOPA DE PUERTO ANGEL

1 medium onion (chopped)
2 cloves garlic (minced)
50g butter
200g tin of Pimiento Morrones (chopped)
2 tomatoes (roasted and sieved)
500ml fish stock (see p36)
pinch of fresh oregano and thyme
1 Bay Leaf
2 small chiles (Guerito or Serrano)
400g Spanish white beans (drained and rinsed)
1 fish fillet (sautéed in butter)
1 dressed crab
250g prawns/shrimps
chopped parsley

Sauté the onion and garlic in butter until soft, add pimientos and tomatoes and sauté for a further 15 minutes then add fish stock, chiles and herbs. Cook for a further 5 minutes then add the beans, cooked fish and crab. Simmer for 10 minutes. Finally add the shrimp/prawns for a quick 1-minute simmer.

Serve garnished with chopped parsley.

Serves 4-6

Soups

CHICKPEA AND CHORIZO SOUP
SOPA DE GARBANZO

1 green Poblano Chile (roasted, peeled and chopped) or use tinned mild green Chile as a substitute
2 medium onions (chopped)
2 cloves garlic (chopped)
50g butter
2 Chorizo sausages
500ml chicken stock (see p35)
1 medium potato (diced)
1 carrot (diced)
2 tins chickpeas
4 tomatoes (roasted and sieved)
4 epazote leaves
chopped parsley for garnish

Sauté the onions, chiles and garlic in butter until soft. Add chicken stock and Chorizo (whole). Add the potato, carrot and chickpeas and simmer for 15 minutes. Remove the cooked Chorizo and dice. Purée the soup and continue to simmer. Add the sieved tomatoes and epazote and simmer for a further 15 minutes. Serve in bowls with some diced Chorizo and chopped parsley sprinkled on top.

Serves 4-6

TWO COOKS AND A SUITCASE

STARTERS
ANTOJITOS

- Pork and Peanut Spread — *page 51*
- Ham Balls In Spicy Mushroom Sauce (Hawg Balls) — *page 51*
- Cajun Popcorn With Creole Sauce — *page 52*
- Crisp Fried Crab Patties — *page 52*
- Fried Provolone Cheese With Creole Sauce — *page 53*
- Stuffed Mushrooms — *page 53*
- Mexican Marinated Fish Cocktail (Ceviche - Puerto Angel) — *page 54*
- Yucatecan Shrimp Cocktail (Coctel de Cameron) — *page 54*
- Little Potato Cakes (Gorditas de Papa - Oaxaca) — *page 55*
- Chorizo Croquettes (Croquetas de Chorizo - Oaxaca) — *page 56*
- Stuffed and Topped Tortillas (Panuchos) — *page 56*
- Cheese Turnovers (Quesadillas) — *page 57*
- Small Fish Tamales (Tamalitos de Pescado) — *page 57*
- Fancy Nachos (Garnachas de Pachuko Cantina) — *page 58*

Starters

PORK AND PEANUT SPREAD

1 tbsp. butter
100g packet peanuts (ground with a rolling pin)
1 medium onion (chopped)
1 clove garlic (crushed)
450g roast pork (seasoned with your favourite Cajun/Creole spice mix)
a pinch sage
a pinch oregano
salt and pepper to taste
juices from the roast pork
parsley to garnish

Roast the seasoned pork in the oven for 50 minutes until tender. When cooled, chop into manageable pieces. Melt the butter in a frying pan, fry the peanuts for 2 minutes then add the onion and garlic and fry for a further 3 minutes. Add the pork, sage, oregano, salt and pepper and the juices from the pork. Mix well and cook for 5 minutes on a low heat. Blend in a food processor if a smoother paste is required. Spread on crackers or thin toast and garnish with parsley.

Serves 6-8

HAM BALLS IN SPICY MUSHROOM SAUCE
HAWG BALLS

HAM BALLS
450g minced ham
225g minced pork
225g Ritz crackers (crushed)
1 egg
150ml milk
cooking oil or lard
1 batch mushroom and peanut sauce (seep37)

Mix ham, pork, crushed crackers and egg, thoroughly. Add the milk a little at a time, just enough to moisten the mixture. Form the mixture into bite-size balls and fry them until brown. Place them on and oven tray and bake on a low to medium heat for 15 minutes. Place on a serving platter, pour over the mushroom sauce and serve pronged with cocktail sticks.

Serves 4

CAJUN POPCORN WITH CREOLE SAUCE

500g shrimps
3 eggs
half pint (225ml) milk
50g maizemeal
50g plain flour
salt and pepper to taste

1 tsp. cayenne pepper
half tsp. garlic powder
1 tsp. sugar
oil for deep frying
half batch of creole sauce (see p37)

Beat eggs and milk together until well blended. Sift all dry ingredients. Pour beaten eggs and milk into the dry ingredients and mix well until a smooth batter is formed. Coat the shrimps in batter. Heat the oil in a deep fat fryer until very hot. Deep fry small quantities of the battered shrimp until crisp. Remove and drain on kitchen roll. Serve immediately with salad and creole sauce (see p37).

Serves 4-6

CRISP FRIED CRAB PATTIES

2 tbsp. olive oil
6 spring onions (finely chopped)
4 stalks celery (finely chopped)
3 cloves garlic (crushed)
dash of Louisiana Hot sauce
qtr. tsp. nutmeg
qtr. tsp. ground ginger
salt and pepper to taste
160g home made breadcrumbs
100ml concentrated beef stock (see p36) or a can of beef consommé

450g crab meat
(arrange a set price with your fishmonger, extracting meat from a crab is best done by experts)
3 hard-boiled eggs (chopped)
1 tbsp. cornflour dissolved in water
4 tbsp. plain flour seasoned with salt and pepper
100g butter for frying

Garnish
salad & lime wedges

Heat the olive oil in a pan and sauté the spring onions, celery and garlic for 3 minutes. Add salt, pepper, and Louisiana hot sauce, nutmeg, ground ginger, breadcrumbs and consommé or stock and mix thoroughly. Stir in the crab meat, eggs and cornflour mixture. Remove from the heat and form into patties, cool and refrigerate for 1/2 an hour. Once cooled dip patties in seasoned flour, lightly fry in butter (in a non-stick pan) until crisp. Serve with garnish.

Serves 4-6.

Starters

FRIED PROVOLONE WITH CREOLE SAUCE

400g Provolone cheese
2 eggs well beaten
1 tsp. salt
half tsp. pepper
few drops Louisiana Hot Sauce
50g breadcrumbs or cracker crumbs
corn or peanut oil
half a batch of creole sauce (see p37)

Cut cheese into sticks approximately 3cm by 8cm. Beat the egg with the hot sauce, salt and pepper. Dip the cheese in egg then coat in breadcrumbs. Shallow fry in corn or peanut oil over a medium heat for a few minutes on each side, until golden brown. Place fried cheese on serving dish and pour over creole sauce. Garnish with salad and parsley.

Serves 4

STUFFED MUSHROOMS

20 medium sized mushrooms
100g butter
1 medium onion (finely chopped)
250g prawns (peeled, cooked and chopped)
salt and pepper to taste
50g breadcrumbs
300ml chicken stock
50g grated Parmesan
2 dressed crabs or 300g frozen crab meat
1 tsp. fresh parsley
25g. butter
1 glass white wine

Remove stems from mushrooms, chop the stems fine and wipe the caps ready for stuffing. Melt 100g of butter in a frying pan, fry the onion and mushroom stems for 5 minutes. Add the chicken stock and bring to the boil, reduce the heat, add prawns and simmer for 1 minute. Remove from heat and stir in the remaining ingredients, except the butter and wine. Stuff the mushrooms with the mixture and place in a greased oven tray. Melt 1 tablespoon of butter in a saucepan, slowly pour in the wine and blend well. Pour this over the stuffed mushrooms and bake in a preheated oven at 175°C for 15-20 minutes.

Serves 4

MEXICAN MARINATED FISH COCKTAIL
CEVICHE - PUERTO ANGEL

300g mackerel fillets (cut into bite sized cubes)
juice of 3 limes
2 cloves garlic (minced)
bunch coriander (chopped)
4 juicy tomatoes (roughly chopped)
1 or 2 tinned Chile Chipotles (chopped)

1 red onion (finely chopped)
salt and pepper to taste
a drizzle of olive oil
pimiento stuffed olives (chopped chunky)
1 avocado (peeled and chopped)
lettuce leaves

Place the fish in glass bowl with the garlic, lime juice and Chile Chipotles. Leave for four hours to allow the acidity of the lime juice to 'cook' the fish. Add everything except lettuce. Toss together, season and serve on lettuce leaves, tostadas or any other tortilla whimsy.

Serves 4-6

YUCATECAN SHRIMP COCKTAIL
COCTEL DE CAMERON

450g bag of peeled shrimp
juice of 2 limes
juice of 1 orange
3 tblsp. olive oil
6 tomatoes (roasted and sieved)
some fresh coriander
1 Chile Habanero

2 cloves garlic, roasted
1 small red onion (chopped)
pinch of allspice
pinch of cumin
salt and pepper
dash of hot sauce
crackers

Fully defrost the shrimp and place in cocktail dishes or glasses.
Place all the liquid ingredients, garlic, coriander and Chile Habanero in a food processor and blend. Add this to the chopped red onion, spices, seasonings and a dash of hot sauce. Mix thoroughly and pour over the shrimp. Leave for one hour and serve with crackers on the side. This is a very liquid marinade. Spoon the shrimp into your anxiously awaiting mouth and drink any remaining liquid.

Many people, myself included, drink shots of tequila with this liquid, treating it like a Sangrita. I refer all Tequila lovers to p137 '**Drinking Tequila**'.

Serves 6

Starters

LITTLE POTATO CAKES
GORDITAS DE PAPA - OAXACA

Pancake Ingredients
4 medium potatoes (peeled, boiled and mashed)
150g Masa Harina
200g Monterey Jack cheese (grated)
fresh coriander (chopped)
1 small onion (grated)
salt and pepper to taste

Topping
Black Refried Beans (see p114)
Pollo Pibil (see p93)
Salsa Fresca (see p39)
sour cream
some fresh coriander
avocado, sliced

Mix all the pancake ingredients in a bowl and knead into firm dough. Form dough into thick discs approximately 8cm wide and 1 cm thick. Shallow fry in oil until crisp and brown on both sides, drain on kitchen paper, top with Refried Black Beans and Pollo Pibil, garnish with salsa, a blob of sour cream, some coriander leaf and slices of avocado.

This makes six large pancakes for a main dish or many cocktail sized ones for canapés.

Many other toppings can be used. Try any of the following:
1. Bean And Picadillo (see p78 + 114)
2. Coctel De Cameron (see p54)
3. Ceviche (see p54)

Serves 6

CHORIZO CROQUETTES
CROQUETAS DE CHORIZO - OAXACA

500g potatoes
1 cooking style Chorizo (boiled and chopped)
chopped parsley
1 egg (beaten)
225g Manchego (grated)
salt and pepper
2 Chile Serrano (minced)
2 eggs (beaten)
home made breadcrumbs
oil for deep frying

Boil the potatoes and mash them. While still warm add the chopped chorizo, parsley, grated cheese, chiles, seasoning and one beaten egg. When the mixture has cooled, form into small sausage shapes. Dip the sausages into the remaining beaten egg and then coat thoroughly with breadcrumbs. Deep-fry the croquettes in hot oil until golden brown. Drain on paper towels and serve with a table salsa and salad garnish.

Serves 4-6

STUFFED AND TOPPED TORTILLAS
PANUCHOS

a portion of Masa dough (see p31)
a portion of Pollo Pibil (shredded off the bone) (see p93)
a portion Refried Black Beans (see p114)
a portion of Yucatan Pickled Onions (see p41)
lettuce (shredded)
tomato (sliced)
avocado (sliced)
Chile Serrano
Feta cheese (crumbled)

Make some extra thick corn tortillas from the masa dough, cook them on a hot griddle, patting them with a spatula as they cook on the second side. This will encourage them to puff up and when they do, carefully cut them open down one side, forming a pocket. Fill the pocket with the beans. When they have all been filled shallow fry them until crisp, and drain on paper towels. Top each with a little of the remaining ingredients, finishing with a sprinkling of feta cheese.

Serves 4-6

Starters

CHEESE TURNOVERS
QUESADILLAS

The Dough
200g Masa Harina
25g plain flour
half tsp. baking powder
butter (melted)
1 egg (beaten)
100ml milk
200g cheese (sliced)
Chile Serrano (minced) or spring onion (chopped)

Mix together the dry dough ingredients. Add the melted butter, egg and milk to form a dough. Separate the dough into small balls, flatten into circles, fill with cheese and chiles or any other filling (see below), and pinch round the edges to seal. Shallow fry in hot oil until golden brown and drain on a kitchen towel. Serve with a homemade salsa or guacamole. Garnish with salad.

TIP: Don't overstuff the quesadillas or the filling will splutter in the hot oil.
VARIATION: Add some chopped, cooked Chorizo to the turnover or try Picadillo (see p78)

Serves 4-6

SMALL FISH TAMALES
TAMALITOS DE PESCADO

A batch of tamale dough (see p32)
24 baby spinach leaves
250g smoked salmon
Chipotle Salsa (see p40)

You can use cut rectangles of banana leaf, cornhusks or Little Buddy's tinfoil tip. For these little tamales the dimension of the foil rectangle should be 8cm by 12cm.

Spread each rectangle with tamale dough, leaving a 1 centimetre gap all round. Top with a spinach leaf - it doesn't matter if it is larger than the dough - and place a piece of smoked salmon on top of the leaf, then a spoonful of Chipotle salsa. Fold into little parcels. Steam for 30 minutes

VARIATION: Try other smoked fish, I especially recommend mackerel.

Serves 4-6

TWO COOKS AND A SUITCASE

FANCY NACHOS
GARNACHAS DE PACHUKO CANTINA

250g bag tortilla chips
250g refried beans

Special Beef Topping
450g stewing steak
1 medium onion
2 Chile Poblano fresh or canned
4 cloves garlic
a dash of sherry
25g tomato puree
250ml water
1 bay leaf
salt and pepper
150g Monterey Jack cheese (grated)

Simmer all the topping ingredients together for 45 minutes until the meat is tender. Blend to a paste in a food processor. Spread each chip with refried beans, then the paste, then sprinkle with cheese. Grill quickly to melt the cheese. Serve immediately. Good as a snack or as a starter.

Serves 4-6

FISH & SEAFOOD

- Salmon With Pistachio Butter — *page 60*
- Fish Fillets in Pecan Sauce — *page 60*
- Trout Stuffed With Crab — *page 61*
- Southern Shrimp Curry — *page 62*
- Simple Coconut Rice — *page 63*
- Shrimp Creole — *page 63*
- Seafood Etoufée — *page 64*
- Yucatan Fish Pie (Pan de Pescado) — *page 65*
- Yucatan Stuffed Crab — *page 66*
- Veracruz Tuna (Atun a la Veracruzana) — *page 67*
- Seafood Enchiladas (Enchiladas de Carabella) — *page 68*
- Fillets of Fish Cooked In Garlic Butter (Filetes Al Mojo de Ajo Especial) — *page 69*
- The Devils Shrimp (Camerones Diablo) — *page 69*
- Fried Fish in Green Tomatillo Sauce (Pescado Frito En Salsa Verde) — *page 70*
- Fishballs in Tomato Sauce (Albondigas de Pescado) — *page 70*

SALMON WITH PISTACHIO BUTTER

4 salmon steaks
(1cm thick, cut along
the length of the fish)
salt and pepper

Pistachio Butter
100g butter
100g pistachio nuts
juice of half a lemon

1 glass very good dry white wine
parsley to garnish
50ml single cream (optional)

To make the pistachio butter, shell and skin the nuts and crush to a powder. Blend nuts with the butter and lemon juice. Melt the pistachio butter in a frying pan over a low heat and; gently sauté the salmon steaks for 10 seconds on each side. Remove steaks to a serving dish. Add the wine to the butter and heat until bubbling. If you want a creamy sauce, reduce heat and gradually add cream to the sauce, being careful not to boil. Pour over the steaks and serve garnished with parsley and sliced lemon. **Serves 4**

FISH FILLETS IN PECAN SAUCE

4 fish fillets (preferably trout)
160g plain flour
2 tsp. cayenne pepper
salt to taste
2 tsp. black pepper
1 egg beaten with 120ml milk
120ml peanut oil
parsley and a lemon

Pecan Sauce
100g broken pecan nuts
3 tbsp. butter
4 dashes Worcester sauce
3 cloves garlic (crushed)
2 dashes Tabasco™ sauce
2 tbsp. fresh lemon juice
salt and pepper to taste

To make the sauce, roast the pecans in the oven at 175ºC for 15 minutes. Cool, and reserve about a third for garnish. Once cooled, chop the remaining pecans in a food processor with the butter, Worcester sauce, Tabasco sauce, lemon juice, garlic, salt and pepper and blend to a paste.

To prepare the fish fillets, mix the flour, salt, pepper and cayenne pepper together thoroughly. Pat each fillet dry with a paper towel. Dip each one into the beaten egg and milk, then into the flour mix, making sure they are completely coated. Heat the peanut oil in a frying pan until hot and fry the fish until golden brown, a few minutes on either side. Transfer the fillets to an oven dish and spread each with the pecan paste then grill until the paste melts. Remove from the grill and garnish with chopped pecans, sliced lemon and sprigs of parsley. Serve immediately. **Serves 4**

Fish & Seafood

TROUT STUFFED WITH CRAB

*1 whole trout per person
(cleaned and boned with the head and tail intact, get your fishmonger to do this)
salt and pepper to taste
juice of half a lemon*

Stuffing
*2 tbsp. butter
1 stalk celery (chopped fine)
1 medium green pepper (chopped fine)
4 spring onions (chopped)
125g crab meat
30g fresh breadcrumbs
2 sprigs parsley
1 egg beaten
140ml sherry
1 tsp. course ground mustard*

*150ml fish stock (see p61)
280ml single cream
parsley*

Dry the fish inside and out with paper towels and then sprinkle the whole fish with salt, pepper and lemon juice. Set aside.
To prepare the stuffing, heat the butter in a saucepan and sauté celery, spring onions and green pepper for 5 minutes until soft. Remove from heat and mix with crabmeat, breadcrumbs, parsley, egg, sherry and mustard. Stuff the fish with the crab mixture and seal with toothpicks. Dot the fish with butter and place in a casserole dish. Put into a preheated oven at 220°C for 15-20 minutes, turning the fish once. The length of time needed depends on the size of fish. Once baked, pour the juices of the fish into a saucepan, add the fish stock, bring to the boil and simmer. Gently stir in the cream to form a sauce, season to taste, pour over the fish and serve immediately. Garnish with chopped parsley.

Variation: After the fish is stuffed you can dip it in egg and a seasoned mixture of cornmeal and flour. Then shallow fry for five minutes on each side until crisp. Serve with creole sauce (see p37)

Stuffing is enough for 4-6 fish, depending on size

SOUTHERN SHRIMP CURRY

1 pineapple (medium sized)
oil for frying
4 spring onions (chopped)
1 stalk celery (chopped)
1 medium green pepper (chopped)
2 cloves garlic (minced)
250ml chicken stock
4 tomatoes (roasted, skinned and chopped)
150ml coconut milk
3 tsp. fresh ginger (crushed)
1 tsp. curry powder (Caribbean is best for this dish)
dash of Louisiana Hot Sauce
salt and pepper
1 tsp. cornflour dissolved in a little water
1kg prawns

Garnish
chopped parsley
lemon slices

Cut the pineapple in half lengthways, cutting through the spiny leaves with a sharp knife. Scoop out most of the fruit and set aside the empty shell halves for filling. Sauté the spring onions, celery, green pepper and garlic in a little oil. When soft add the chicken stock, tomatoes, coconut milk, ginger, curry powder, hot sauce and 100g of pineapple fruit. Season with salt and pepper. Simmer for 15-20 minutes to blend the flavours and reduce the sauce. Add the prawns and cook for 30-60 seconds depending on the size of the prawns. Place the pineapple shells in a preheated oven for 10 minutes, then pour the shrimp curry into the shells. Serve the filled shells on a platter of coconut rice (see p63), pouring the extra curry over the shells to allow the sauce to overflow onto the rice. Garnish with chopped parsley and slices of lemon. Let everyone help themselves to curry and rice.

Serves 4 -6

Fish & Seafood

SIMPLE COCONUT RICE

250g Thai fragrant rice
200ml chicken stock
100ml coconut milk
handful of chopped fresh coriander
salt and pepper to taste

Combine the rice, chicken stock and coconut milk in a saucepan over a medium heat. When liquid starts to boil stir once and reduce heat to very low, cover and cook for 20 minutes. No peeking! Turn off heat and fluff up rice, adding chopped coriander. Present on the platter with the pineapple halves filled with curry.

Serves 4

SHRIMP CREOLE

50g butter
25g plain flour
4 spring onions (chopped)
1 green pepper (chopped)
1 stalk celery (chopped)
2 cloves garlic (minced)
1 can chopped tomatoes
250ml fish stock
150g Pancetta (chopped into small pieces and pan fried)
pinch thyme
2 bay leaves
splash Worcester sauce
juice from a qtr. lemon
Louisiana Hot Sauce to taste
salt and pepper
1kg shrimp or prawns (defrosted if frozen)
parsley garnish
lemon wedges

Make a light roux using the flour and butter (see p27). When cooked, add the onions, green pepper, celery and garlic and stir briefly. Cool the roux down by adding the tomatoes, then the fish stock, spices, Worcester sauce, lemon juice, hot sauce, seasoning and pan-fried Pancetta. Simmer to reduce the sauce, about 15-20 minutes. Throw in the shrimp and cook for 30-60 seconds depending on the size, don't be tempted to cook the shrimp longer as they go rubbery. Garnish with parsley and lemon wedges. Serve with rice.

Variation: Make a batch of creole sauce (see p37). Pan-fry the shrimp in garlic butter, remove to a serving dish and smother with the creole sauce. Serve as above, garnished with parsley and lemon over rice.

Serves 4-6

SEAFOOD ETOUFFÉE

Dark Roux (see p27)
50g butter
25g plain flour

2 stalks celery (chopped)
1 green pepper (chopped)
4 spring onions (chopped)
2 cloves garlic (chopped)
250ml chicken stock
salt and pepper
half tsp. cayenne pepper

1 tbsp. Worcester sauce
thyme
parsley
bay leaf
1kg mix of scallops
large peeled prawns
dressed crab
small carton cream
parsley to garnish

extra Louisiana Hot Sauce (optional)

Make a dark roux with the flour and butter (see p27), add the chopped vegetables and cook for 5 minutes to soften. Slowly stir in the stock, add herbs and seasoning, simmer for 35 minutes. Add seafood and cook for 2-3 minutes. Stir in cream, serve over boiled rice and garnish with sprigs of parsley. Add some hot sauce if desired.

Serves 4-6

Fish & Seafood

YUCATAN FISH PIE
PAN DE PESCADO

500g cod or other
100ml fish stock
2 cloves garlic (roasted and mashed)
2 sprigs epazote
salt and pepper to taste
4 allspice berries (crushed)
12 thick home-made tortillas - Panuchos (see p31)
Black Refried Beans (see p114)
1 batch Chiltomate Sauce (see p38)

Garnish
lime wedges
pickled onions (see p41)
Chile Serrano flowers (see p28)
2 hard-boiled eggs (finely chopped)
chopped parsley

Poach the fish in stock with garlic, epazote, allspice berries, salt and pepper. Once the fish is cooked remove and flake. Use the stock to make Chiltomate sauce. Stuff the tortillas with the flaked fish and black beans. Put one layer in a casserole dish, smother with the special Chiltomate sauce, place another layer of stuffed tortillas and finish with more sauce. Bake for 15 minutes to heat through. Garnish with pickled onions, lime wedges, Chile Serrano flowers, chopped eggs and parsley.

Variation: If you find cutting open the Tortillas and stuffing a bit tricky, then just top the Tortilla instead of filling. You can also do a **Tamale Pie** version (see p33)

Serves 4-6

YUCATAN STUFFED CRAB

4 dressed crabs (keep shells)

Stuffing
25g butter
4 spring onions (chopped)
2 cloves garlic (minced)
12 capers
40g raisins
12 pimiento stuffed olives
2 Chile Serrano (chopped)
2 hard-boiled eggs (chopped)
4 tomatoes (roasted, peeled and sieved)
handful of parsley (chopped)
a few strands of saffron
half tsp. cinnamon
salt and pepper to taste

Topping
breadcrumbs
25g butter

For the stuffing melt the butter in a pan and sauté the garlic and onions until soft. Add the rest of the stuffing ingredients and mix well. Spoon the mixture into the crab shells, sprinkle with breadcrumbs, put a knob of butter on top of the breadcrumbs and bake until golden brown.

Serves 4

TWO COOKS AND A SUITCASE

VERACRUZ TUNA
ATUN A LA VERACRUZANA

4 or 6 tuna fish steaks (thinly cut, gently flattened and seasoned with salt and pepper)
juice of 2 limes

Sauce
oil for frying
2 cloves garlic (chopped)
2 onions (chopped)
500g tomatoes (roasted, peeled and sieved)
250ml fish stock
12 pimiento stuffed olives (sliced)
1 pimiento (chopped)
6 capers
pinch of thyme
pinch of marjoram
2 bay leaves
2 Chile de Arbol or 2 Chile Serrano (chopped fine)
salt and pepper to taste

For Frying Fish
25g butter
2 cloves garlic (finely chopped)

Garnish
chopped parsley
lime wedges
olives

Marinade the seasoned fillets in limejuice for an hour, and meanwhile make the sauce. In a little oil, sauté the onions and garlic until soft, add the tomatoes and fish stock, add the remaining ingredients and simmer the sauce for 15-20 minutes.

Heat the butter and garlic in a large frying pan and cook the tuna steak very quickly - 20 seconds on either side. Keep warm on a serving plate. Pour over the finished sauce and garnish with chopped parsley, lime wedges and some whole olives.

Serves 4-6

SEAFOOD ENCHILADAS
ENCHILADAS DE CARABELLA

The Fish
25g butter
4 cloves garlic (crushed)
4 spring onions or shallots (chopped)
200g white fish (cut into bite sized chunks)
150g scallops
150g cooked prawns
1 dressed crab
4 tomatoes (roasted and sieved)
pinch of cumin
salt and pepper
juice of half a lime
fresh coriander (chopped)

The Sauce
25g butter
1 onion (chopped)
3 cloves garlic (chopped)
250ml fish or chicken stock (see p35 + 36)
6 tomatoes (roasted, peeled and sieved)
2 New Mexico Red chiles (fresh or dried)
50ml single cream

Garnish
crumbled Cheshire or Feta cheese
boiled egg cut into wedges
coriander leaf

1 batch home made corn tortillas (see p31), or bought corn or flour tortillas.

Melt the butter and sauté garlic and spring onion until soft. Add the fish fillets and scallops. Continue cooking for one minute and add the cooked seafood, tomatoes, cumin, salt, pepper, lime juice and coriander. Cook gently to blend the flavours for a few minutes.

Fill each tortilla with the seafood mixture. Put each filled tortilla on an ovenproof platter, smother with red enchilada sauce, and bake for 20 minutes at 180°C. Garnish with crumbled cheese, wedges of boiled egg and coriander leaf.

The Sauce
Sauté the garlic and onion in the butter until soft. Add the stock, tomatoes, chiles and seasoning, and simmer for about 15 minutes to reduce the sauce. Slowly add the single cream and remove from heat.

Serves 4-6

FILLETS OF FISH COOKED IN GARLIC BUTTER
FILETES AL MOJO DE AJO ESPECIAL

4 or 6 of your favourite fish fillets
salt and pepper
juice of 2 limes
25g butter
4 cloves garlic (minced)

enough mayonnaise to thinly spread over each fillet
200g tin pimientos (cut into strips)
12 pimiento stuffed olives (sliced)
chopped parsley
lemon or lime slices

Season fish fillets with salt and pepper, pour the lime juice over, and leave to marinade for an hour. Heat the butter in a frying pan with the garlic, cook each fillet for one minute on each side - thicker fillets may take longer. Place the fillets on a serving platter, spread thinly with mayonnaise, sprinkle with parsley and decorate with pimiento strips and olive slices. Finish with a slice of lemon on each fillet. Serve immediately.

Serves 4-6

THE DEVIL'S SHRIMP
CAMERONES DIABLO

The Sauce
some olive oil for frying
2 onions (chopped)
2 cloves garlic (chopped)
500g tomatoes (roasted, peeled and sieved)
1 can of Coke or Fanta
2 Chile Chipotle (chopped fine)
2 Chile de Arbol (chopped fine)
salt and pepper

500g shrimp (whole fresh ones or frozen if they are out of season)
25g butter for frying
4 cloves garlic
salt and pepper

parsley to garnish
lime wedges

To make the sauce, sauté the onions and garlic in a little oil until soft. Add the sieved tomatoes, Coke or Fanta, chiles, salt and pepper. Simmer the sauce until thick, 15-20 minutes.
Sauté the garlic in the butter, add the shrimp and cook until pink. Season with salt and pepper, add the Chile sauce, mix well, and serve sprinkled with parsley and wedges of lime. Serve with rice.

Variations: try using other seafood.

Serves 4-6

FRIED FISH IN GREEN TOMATILLO SAUCE
PESCADO FRITO EN SALSA VERDE

8 cod fillets
salt and pepper
juice of 2 limes
4 cloves garlic (crushed)
2 tblsp. fresh coriander (finely chopped)

1 egg (beaten)
home-made breadcrumbs

oil for frying

1 batch Salsa Verde (see p40)

100g Feta or Wensleydale cheese
some chopped coriander.

Mix together lime juice, garlic, coriander, salt and pepper. Rub this mixture into the fish fillets. Dip the fillets in egg and breadcrumbs and fry quickly until brown on both sides. Serve on plates, pour over Salsa Verde, sprinkle with a crumbly white cheese (feta or Wensleydale) and chopped coriander.

Serves 4-6

FISHBALLS IN TOMATO SAUCE
ALBONDIGAS DE PESCADO

Fishballs

500g whitefish fillets - haddock or hake are both good
(finely chopped)
1 spring onion (chopped)
1 tomato (roasted and sieved)
a handful of chopped parsley
2 slices of bread (crusts removed, soaked in vinegar and water and squeezed dry)
2 eggs
your favourite hot sauce to taste
salt and pepper

Masa Harina
oil for shallow frying
1 batch tomato sauce (see p38)

Garnish

fresh Poblano chiles (roasted, peeled and cut into strips)
boiled egg (chopped fine)
olives
parsley

Blend all the fishball ingredients in a food processor to form a paste. Shape into balls and chill in the fridge for 1 hour. When chilled, roll in Masa Harina and shallow fry until crisp and golden. Drain on kitchen paper.
Serve smothered in tomato sauce, garnished with strips of Chile Poblano, sliced olives, chopped egg and parsley.
Variations: This recipe works well with Salsa Verde (see p40), Salsa Chipotle (see p40) or Yucatan Chiltomate Sauce (see p38).

Serves 4-6

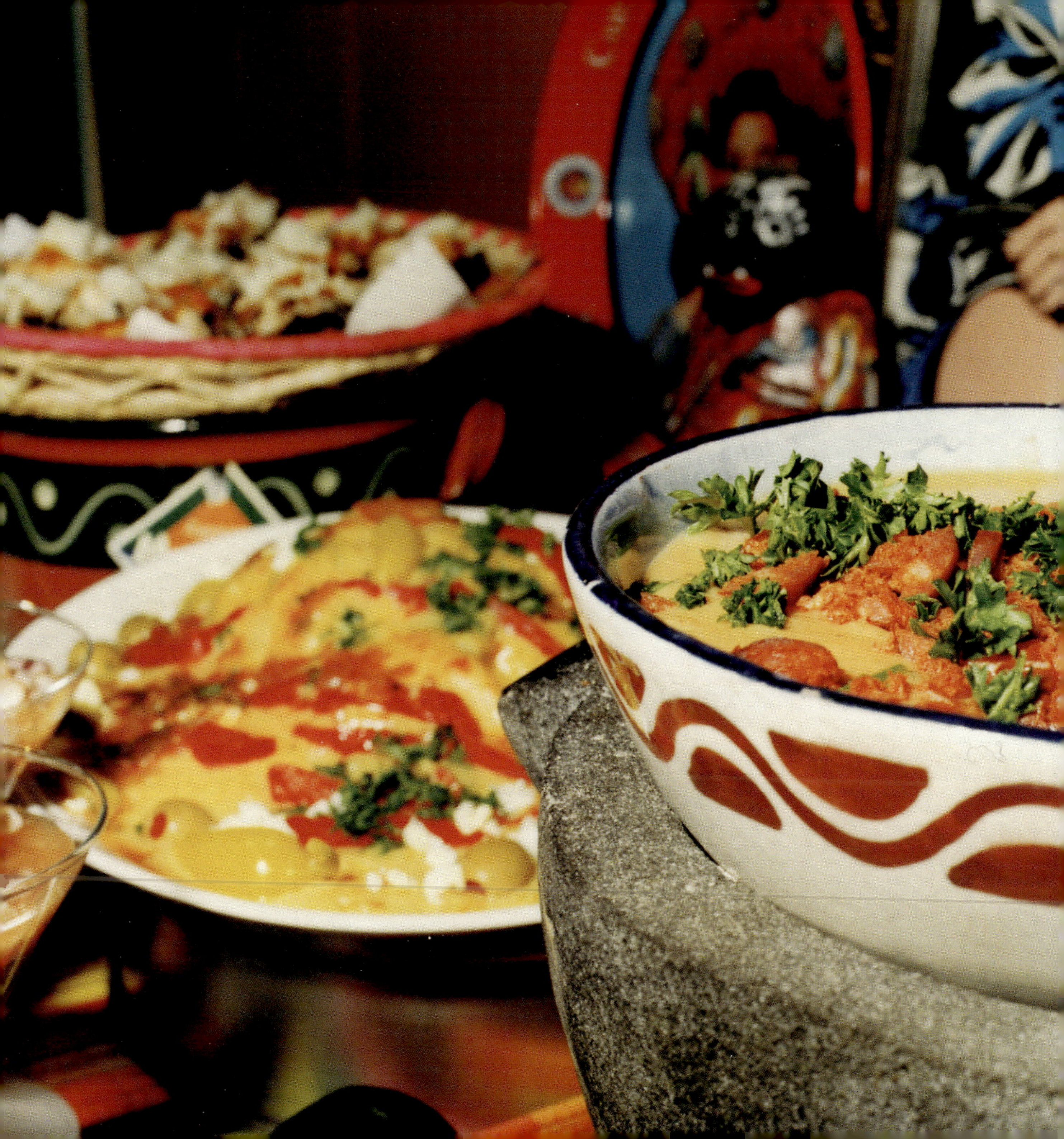

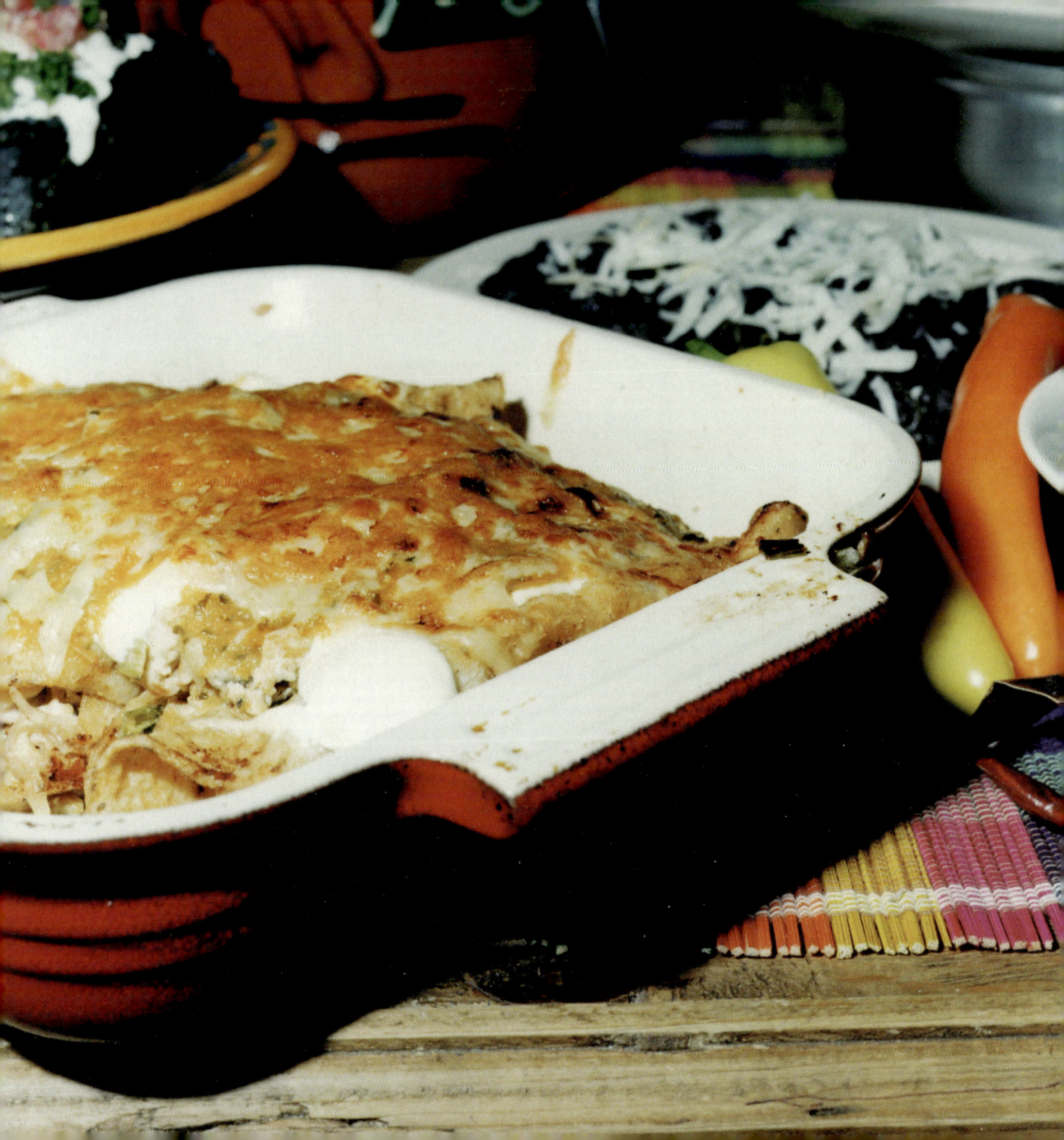

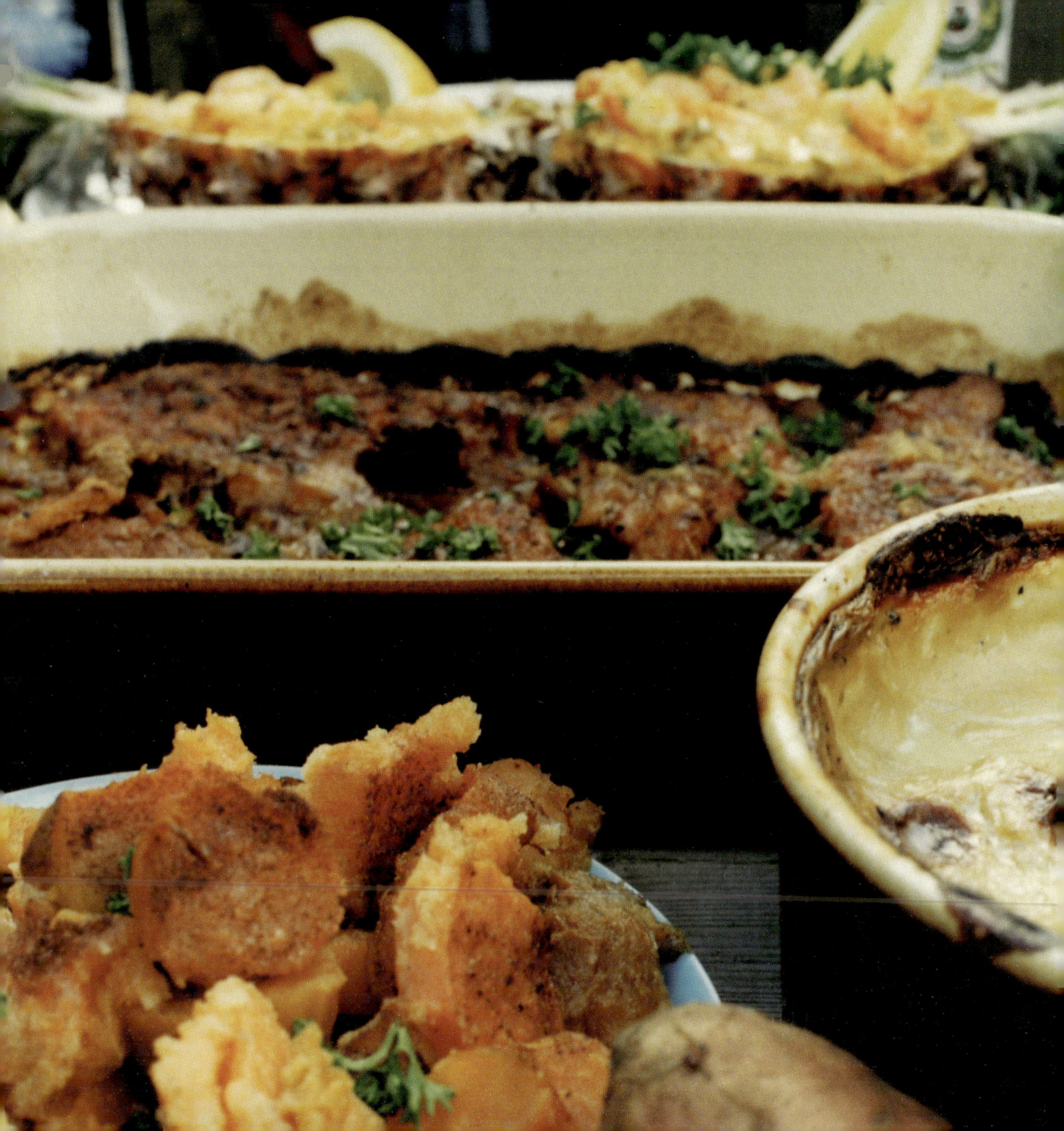

Corona
Don't Forgetta Mezzetta
Mezzetta
HERRADURA
BLANCO
IMPORTADO
El Te
de Don F
100% BLUE AGAVE TEQ

MEAT

- Little Buddy's Creole Stuffed Pork Chops — page 72
- Pork Medallions With Mushroom Sauce — page 72
- Sister Alberta's Smothered Poke Chops — page 73
- Marcus Frasier's Chicken Fried Steak — page 73
- Cabbage Roll (Soulfood) — page 74
- Mark Garcy's Savoury Pie — page 75
- Bob The Chef's BBQ Ribs — page 76
- Beef Fillets With Marchand de Vin Sauce — page 77
- Stuffed Cheese (Queso Relleno - Valladolid) — page 78
- Meatballs In Smoked Chipotle Sauce (Albondigas en Salsa de Chipotle) — page 79
- Fried Pork Mexican Style (Milanesa de Villahermosa) — page 80
- Shredded Pork Tacos (Carnitas de Oaxaca) — page 81
- Real Authentic Mexican Chile From Oaxaca (Chile Con Carne Oaxacqueño) — page 82
- Roast Pork Yucatan Style (Conchinita Pibil) — page 83
- Stuffed Chiles (1) (Chile Relleno (1)) — page 84
- Stuffed Chiles (2) (Chile Relleno (2)) — page 85
- Stuffed Pork Fillet Yucatan Style (Cerdo Enrollado) — page 86

LITTLE BUDDY'S CREOLE STUFFED PORK CHOPS

4 or 6 thick cut pork chops
(flatten the meat part, not the fat, with a meat hammer
and cut a pocket in the pork chops down to the bone,
through the fat)

The Sauce
juices from the cooked pork
250ml beef or chicken stock (see p35)
100ml single cream

Stuffing
breadcrumbs
1 stalk celery (finely chopped)
1 green pepper (finely chopped)
1 apple (peeled, cored and finely chopped)
2 spring onions (finely chopped)
50g raisins
dash Worcester sauce
dash hot sauce
1 egg beaten
salt and pepper to taste

For the stuffing, mix all the ingredients together in a bowl, thoroughly. Open the pockets of each pork chop and stuff with this mixture. Close the opening with toothpicks. Seal the pork chops by frying in a little oil, about 3 minutes on each side. Place the chops in an oven dish with a little water, cover and bake for 45 minutes at gas mark 4. After half an hour cooking, drain the juices from the pork chops into a saucepan, and return the chops covered to the oven. To the juices add the stock and simmer for 15 minutes to reduce. Stir in the cream – do not boil. Remove the chops from the oven and place on a serving dish. Drizzle the sauce over and serve with Cornbread (see p112) and Scalloped Potatoes (see p102).

Serves 4-6

PORK MEDALLIONS WITH MUSHROOM SAUCE

1 pork tenderloin
4 tbsp. cider vinegar
4 dashes Louisiana Hot Sauce
salt and pepper to taste
50g butter

1 batch Mushroom and
Peanut Sauce (see p37)

Garnish
fresh chopped parsley

Cut the pork into medallions. Marinade in the vinegar, hot sauce, salt and pepper. Now make the Mushroom and Peanut Sauce (see p37).

Pan-fry the medallions in butter until golden brown on both sides (about 3 minutes on either side). Pour the sauce over the medallions, stir to blend, and simmer for a couple of minutes. Remove the medallions to a serving platter and pour over the sauce. Garnish with chopped parsley.

Serves 4

SISTER ALBERTA'S SMOTHERED POKE CHOPS

8 thin cut boneless pork chops

Spice Mixture
mix together
1tsp. onion salt
1tsp. salt
half tsp. cayenne pepper
half tsp. oregano
half tsp. mustard powder

flour seasoned with salt and pepper
enough oil for shallow frying

The Gravy
half tblsp. plain flour
1 medium onion (finely chopped)
250ml chicken stock or creole beef stock
(see p35 Or 36)

Hammer the chops, to tenderise. Season with spice mixture, by throwing the pork chops into a bag containing the seasoned flour and shaking well to coat each chop. Shake off the excess flour. Heat oil to high temperature (not smoking), and place chops in the hot oil four at a time. Fry for 5 minutes, then carefully flip over to fry the other side. When well-browned, remove chops to an oven dish and keep warm. Drain all but 1 tablespoon of the oil and the brown crispy bits from the frying. Add the flour and stir constantly over a low heat for 10 minutes to form a roux. Add onion and cook until soft, then slowly stir in the stock to form a gravy season with salt and pepper. Smother the chops with gravy and bake covered for 25 minutes until chops are tender.
Serve with Baked Macaroni (see p111) or Mashed Potatoes and Black-eyed Peas (see p109).

Serves 4

MARCUS FRASIER'S CHICKEN FRIED STEAK

enough oil for shallow frying
4 frying-beef steaks
salt and pepper
1 tsp. paprika (Spanish Pimenton)
2 cloves garlic (crushed)
1 egg beaten with 1 tbsp. milk
1 cup cornmeal mixed with 100g crushed Ritz crackers

Season steaks with salt, pepper and paprika and rub them with the crushed garlic. Flatten steaks with a meat hammer. This will pound in the seasonings and tenderise the meat at the same time. Dip the steaks in the egg mixture then into the cornmeal mixture, thoroughly coating both sides. Heat the oil (medium hot) in a frying pan and cook the steaks until golden brown, about 3 minutes on each side. Serve with your favourite Black-eyed Peas and Baked Macaroni (see p109 + 111).

Serves 4

CABBAGE ROLL
SOULFOOD

The Stuffing
200g minced beef
200g minced pork
3 spring onions (finely chopped)
200g cooked rice
4 cloves garlic (crushed)
1 tsp. dried sage
2 tsp. oregano
1 tsp. cayenne pepper
salt and pepper to taste
150g crackers (Ritz or TUC crushed in a mixer)
1 egg beaten

1 large cabbage
oil for frying

The Sauce
portion of creole sauce (see p37) or
creole mushroom & peanut sauce
(see p37).

Remove as many whole large leaves from the cabbage as possible, (use the small ones for soup or coleslaw). Soak the leaves in boiled salted water to soften them. Mix all the stuffing ingredients together. Take a cabbage leaf, stuff it, roll it, tucking in the ends to form a neat parcel, and fix the seams with a toothpick. Continue until all the stuffing is used. Heat the oil in a frying pan and lightly fry all the cabbage rolls, a few at a time. Place in a casserole dish, cover with your chosen sauce, and bake for 20 minutes at 190°C. Serve with your favourite Soulfood vegetable dishes.

Serves 6

MARK GARCY'S SAVOURY PIE

The Crust
200g canned Spanish Tomate Frito (half a can)
(you can substitute passata if you must)
450g steak mince
1 small onion (finely chopped)
1 green pepper (finely chopped)
100g French bread crumbs (half French stick,
heated in the oven and crushed into crumbs)
1 egg beaten
half tsp. Spanish paprika (pimenton)
salt and pepper to taste

The Stuffing
1 400g can Spanish haricot beans or pinto beans
(drained and rinsed)
200g canned Tomate Frito (half a can)
2 cups cooked rice
20g Texas chilli seasoning
salt & pepper to taste

Garnish
sour cream
crumbled Feta cheese
chopped parsley

Mix together all the ingredients for the crust. It is best to do this by hand so the meat is well combined. Once mixed, turn out into a well greased deep pie dish and line the bottom and sides with the mixture as you would with pastry. The meat is the shell.

Mix together all the ingredients for the stuffing and fill the pie shell with this. Cover with tin foil and bake at 180ºC for 25 minutes. Remove from the oven and garnish with sour cream, crumbled Feta and chopped parsley.

Serves 6

BOB THE CHEF'S BBQ RIBS

BBQ Sauce
50g butter
2 medium onions (finely chopped)
3 tbsp. tomato ketchup
3 tbsp. brown sugar
3 tbsp. cider vinegar
2 tbsp. Worcester sauce
juice of half a lemon
250ml meat stock (see p36)
2 tsp. mild American mustard
salt and pepper to taste
Louisiana Hot Sauce

4 sheets of pork ribs seasoned with salt, pepper and paprika
4 cloves garlic (crushed)
a few drops of liquid smoke

Garnish
some fresh parsley

For the sauce, melt the butter and sauté the onions for 10 minutes until soft. Add the rest of the ingredients and simmer for 20 minutes.

Marinate the ribs in the sauce for a few hours or overnight then place them in an oven dish, cover and bake for 1 & a half hours at 160°C. Baste the ribs with the sauce every half an hour. After the 1 & a half hours, drain the sauce into a saucepan and simmer for 20 minutes to reduce. Meanwhile, return the ribs to the oven and cook uncovered at 200°C to brown them, for about 10 minutes. Serve the ribs smothered in the reduced BBQ sauce. Garnish with parsley and serve with coleslaw and cornbread.

Note: the final ten minutes of cooking works even better on an outdoor BBQ.

Variation: this BBQ sauce works well with chicken and pork chops.

Serves 4

BEEF FILLETS WITH MARCHAND DE VIN SAUCE

4-6 beef fillets (seasoned with salt and pepper)
25g butter for frying

Marchand de Vin Sauce
50g butter
30g plain flour
1 stalk celery (finely chopped)
4 spring onions (finely chopped)
1 green pepper (finely chopped)
50g mushrooms (finely chopped)
2 cloves garlic (crushed)
6 medium tomatoes (chopped)
250ml creole beef stock (see p36)
half a bottle of red wine
2 sprigs fresh thyme
2 bay leaves
salt and pepper to taste

Garnish
some fresh parsley

Marchand de Vin Sauce
Make a light roux with the butter and flour (see p27). Stir vegetables into the roux stirring for a few minutes, then stir in the stock, red wine, tomatoes, herbs, salt and pepper. Simmer for 30 minutes to blend the flavours. Drain through a sieve, squeezing all the juice out of the vegetable mixture. Reserve the rich stock.

Melt the butter in a pan and fry the seasoned fillet steaks to your liking. Add the strained Marchand de Vin sauce to the pan and stir round the steaks in the sauce, making sure that all the pan juices from frying the steaks are incorporated into the sauce. Place the steaks on a serving dish and drizzle the sauce over. Garnish with chopped parsley.

Serves 4-6

STUFFED CHEESE
QUESO RELLENO - VALLADOLID

1 Edam cheese brushed with oil

Picadillo
oil for frying
50g bacon (chopped)
1 large onion (finely chopped)
4 cloves garlic (crushed)
500g minced pork
1 Chile Guajillo (soaked and pulp removed)
1 Chile Poblano (chopped) (a green pepper can be substituted)
50g raisins
150g almonds (roasted and ground to powder)
4 tomatoes (roasted, skinned and sieved)
12 pimiento stuffed olives (sliced)
half tsp. dried epazote
1 tsp. ground allspice berries
salt and pepper to taste

The Sauce
50g butter
25g flour
100ml milk
150ml chicken stock (see p35)
small bunch of epazote (substitute bay leaves)
6 capers
12 stoned green olives
pinch of saffron
hot yellow chiles (Chile Guerito or substitute)
some of the scooped out Edam (grated)
4 tomatoes (roasted, peeled then blended)

Garnish
Chiltomate Sauce (see p38)
Pickled Red Onions (see p41)
shredded lettuce
radish flowers (see p28)

Cut the top of the Edam cheese, about qtr. way down. Scoop out the cheese leaving a 1 & a half cm thick wall, top and bottom.

Make the Picadillo. Sauté the bacon, onion and garlic until soft, add the pork and brown well. Add the remaining ingredients and simmer until cooked, about 25 minutes. Season to taste and stir regularly to prevent sticking. You may have to add a little water from time to time to prevent sticking. Fill the cheese bottom and top with the Picadillo, join both sides together, and wrap in a towel, tying the gathered end of the cloth with string. Place in a steamer and steam for 10-15 minutes (enough time to start melting the cheese).

To make the sauce, melt the butter in a saucepan and stir in the flour. Cook, stirring constantly for a couple of minutes, then slowly stir in the milk to form a white sauce. Add the chicken stock and the rest of the ingredients and simmer for 10-15 minutes to form a cheesy white sauce.

Remove the cheese and place on a serving dish. Smother with special white sauce then spoon over some Chiltomate sauce. Garnish the sides of the platter with lots of shredded salad, olives, pickled red onions and radish flowers.

Serves 4-6

MEATBALLS IN SMOKED CHIPOTLE SAUCE
ALBONDIGAS EN SALSA DE CHIPOTLE

Meatballs
225g minced pork
225g minced beef
1 small onion (grated or very finely chopped)
150g breadcrumbs + 25g Masa Harina
4 cloves garlic (toasted and minced)
1 tsp. cumin
1 tsp. Mexican oregano
1 tblsp. tomato purée
salt and pepper to taste
2 eggs

The Sauce
25g butter
1 onion (chopped)
2 cloves garlic (crushed)
500g fresh tomatoes (roasted, peeled and sieved)
250ml chicken stock (see p35)
2 Chile Chipotles (from a tin of Chipotles in adobo sauce, use some adobo sauce as well)
2 tbsp. peanut butter

Garnish
sour cream
chopped roasted peanuts
some coriander

The Sauce
Sauté the onions and garlic in a little butter until soft, then add tomatoes and chicken stock. Add Chile Chipotles and some adobo sauce, and simmer for 20 minutes stirring occasionally. Stir in the peanut butter in the last couple of minutes. Blend the sauce with a food processor or hand held blender.

For the meatballs, thoroughly mix all the ingredients together with your hands, in a bowl, and roll into bite size balls. Place the meatballs on a well-greased baking sheet and bake in a hot oven (200°C) for 15 minutes. Turn them every 5 minutes to ensure all round cooking. When ready, place meatballs in a casserole dish, pour over Chipotle Sauce and bake for a further 15 minutes. Garnish with a blob of sour cream, chopped roast peanuts and a little coriander. Serve with rice.

Serves 4-6

FRIED PORK MEXICAN STYLE
MILANESA DE VILLAHERMOSA

1 pork fillet (cut into four steaks and flatten or get your butcher to do it)
1 tbsp. cider vinegar
2 dried Chile Guajillo (re-hydrated, seeded and pulp extracted) (see p28 - 29)
2 cloves garlic (crushed)
salt and pepper to taste
oil for shallow frying
1 egg (beaten)

Seasoned Flour
mix together
100g flour
100g Masa Harina
salt and pepper

Chipotle Mayo
mix together
200g jar mayonnaise
1 Chile Chipotle (finely chopped)
juice of half a lime
pinch of fresh chopped parsley

Mix the vinegar, garlic, Chile pulp, salt and pepper into a thin paste, and rub into the flattened pork steaks. Marinate for at least 1 hour. Dip steaks into seasoned flour and let stand for 10 minutes. Then dip each steak in egg and back into the flour mixture. Shake off excess flour and shallow fry in hot oil until golden brown on both sides. Drain on kitchen towel. Serve with a dollop of Chipotle Mayonnaise and your favourite Mexican side dish.

Serves 4

SHREDDED PORK TACOS
CARNITAS DE OAXACA

This is probably the original dish that Tex Mex Fajitas was based on.

1kg diced pork shoulder (bite size pieces)
2 medium onions (finely chopped)
100g butter (2x50g)
small glass of sherry
salt and pepper to taste

Presentation
whole crisp lettuce leaves
freshly made guacamole (see p39)
a load of tortillas (flour or corn)
chopped parsley
bottle of hot sauce for the table
a bunch of friends
1 crate Mexican beer

Place the pork in a large frying pan, making sure the pork cubes are in one single layer. Cover with water, and add seasoning. Bring to the boil then reduce to a low simmer. Keep a close eye on the pork, and when the water runs dry start turning the meat in it's own juices until it starts to brown. Add some boiling water from a kettle, just enough to cover the pork, and start the process again. When the water runs dry this time add the onions and 50g butter. Frying the pork and onions together, repeat the process, adding some sherry. When the water and sherry runs dry this time add the other 50g butter and adjust the seasoning to taste. Fry until meat is well browned and all the water is gone. Place on a serving platter, garnish with chopped parsley, and surround with crisp lettuce leaves. Have the guacamole, hot sauce and warmed tortillas on the table.

To consume, take a lettuce leaf, spoon in some meat, guacamole and hot sauce. Roll the filled leaf in a tortilla pancake, have a beer handy and enjoy.

Serves 6-8

REAL AUTHENTIC MEXICAN CHILE FROM OAXACA
CHILE CON CARNE OAXAQUENO

some oil for frying
500g pork (diced)
2 medium onions (finely chopped)
4 cloves garlic (crushed)
4 tomatoes (roasted and sieved)
150ml freshly squeezed orange juice
2 tsp. vinegar
1 bay leaf
1 tsp. oregano
2 Chile Anchos (pulp extracted, see p28 - 29)
3 Chile Guajillo
2 tblsp. toasted breadcrumbs
2 corn tortillas or a handful of crushed tortilla chips
25g toasted almonds
2 tsp. sesame seeds
3 cooking Chorizo sausages (chopped and sautéed)
500g can of cooked black beans (optional)

Sauté the onions and garlic in oil until soft, add pork and brown well. Add the tomatoes, orange juice, spices, vinegar and Chile pulps and simmer for 45 minutes until pork is tender. In a food processor blend the almonds, sesame seeds, tortillas and breadcrumbs and add to the stew along with the cooked Chorizo and black beans. Simmer for 15 minutes to blend flavours.

Serves 6-8

YUCATAN STYLE PORK
CONCHINITA PIBIL

Recado De Achiote
3 tblsp. annato seeds (ground)
12 allspice berries
2 tsp. Mexican oregano
half tsp. cumin
6 cloves garlic
1 tbsp. cider vinegar
juice of half a grapefruit, 1 orange and 1 lime

or if you can get an Achiote cube, simply mix it with the fruit juices.

2.5 kg joint of pork shoulder (well seasoned with salt and pepper)
2 Chile Guerito or Banana Wax (chopped)
1 kg tomatoes (chopped)
2 tblsp. fresh coriander (chopped)

To make the Recado de Achiote, blend all the ingredients together in a spice grinder or mortar and pestle to form a paste. Mix this with the fruit juices to form a meat marinade. Rub the marinade thoroughly into the pork, making sure it's well covered all over. Marinate for several hours or overnight.

Wrap the pork tightly in banana leaves. If not available then use tin foil. Place in a large casserole dish with a few cups of water. Cover, and slowly bake for 3 & half - 4 hours at gas mark 4.

Remove the pork from the package. Shred the meat and keep it warm. Simmer the pan juices with the chopped Chile, coriander and tomatoes. Reduce to form a sauce, and pour over the shredded meat. Serve with plenty of tortillas and Yucatan pickled onions (see p41).

Serves 8-10

STUFFED CHILES (1)
CHILE RELLENO (1)

6 fresh Poblano chiles or canned ones
1 portion Picadillo for stuffing (see p78)

Garnish
crumbled Cheshire or Wensleydale cheese
chopped parsley

2 eggs separated
100g plain flour seasoned with salt & pepper
oil for shallow frying

Tomato Sauce
oil for frying
1 onion (finely chopped)
2 cloves garlic (crushed)
6 tomatoes (roasted, peeled and sieved)
250ml chicken stock (see p35)
1 tsp. brown sugar
qtr. tsp. allspice
handful of chopped parsley
salt and pepper
4 leaves fresh basil (finely chopped)

Tomato Sauce
Sauté the onions and garlic until soft, then add the tomatoes. Stir in the chicken stock, sugar, allspice and parsley. Season with salt and pepper and simmer for 15 minutes. Stir in the basil leaves. Place in a blender and blend to a smooth sauce.

If using fresh Poblanos, place them on a sheet of tin foil and grill, turning each Chile until the skin is brown and blistered all over. Wrap the tin foil round the peppers and leave to sweat for 10 minutes. Remove the skin carefully and make a cut down the side of each pepper. Gently remove the seeds and inner stalk. Stuff each pepper with Picadillo, roll peppers in seasoned flour, and set aside. Beat the egg yolks. Beat the egg whites until stiff and gently fold into the egg yolks. Dip each pepper into the egg mixture. Heat oil in a frying pan until hot and gently lower the peppers into it. Fry until golden brown all over. Drain on kitchen towel. Place peppers on a big serving dish, or individual plates, pour over the tomato sauce and sprinkle with crumbled cheese and parsley.

Note: Canned Poblanos come peeled, with seeds and pith removed. Very handy for this dish. Fill them as best you can and squeeze the Chile round the filling, then dip in flour and egg.
Variations: Cream Cheese, Shredded Chicken, Refried Beans, Shredded Pork all work well as fillings.

Serves 6

STUFFED CHILES (2) - THE SALAD VERSION
CHILE RELLENAS (2)

6 small Poblano chiles (roasted, peeled and de-seeded as in previous recipe) or canned and ready to use.
1 portion Picadillo (see p78)

Sauce
100g crème fraiche
100g walnuts or pecans (finely chopped)
1 tbsp. chopped parsley
salt and pepper

Dressing
50ml olive oil
25ml cider vinegar
juice of half a lime
salt and pepper

Garnish
shredded lettuce
sliced hard boiled egg
strips of pimiento
pomegranate seeds
chopped parsley

Stuff the peppers with Picadillo then bake in a preheated oven at 200°C for 15 minutes. Place baked Chiles on a serving platter and allow to cool. Mix together all the ingredients for the dressing and blend well. Once the chiles are cool drizzle the dressing over them. Mix crème fraiche with pecans, parsley, salt and pepper and pour this over the peppers. Surround the stuffed peppers with shredded lettuce, sliced egg, strips of pimiento, pomegranate seeds and chopped parsley.

Serve cold as a starter for 6 or main dish for 2-3

STUFFED PORK FILLET YUCATAN STYLE
CERDO ENROLLADO

2 whole pork fillets
tblsp. Recado de Achiote (see p83)
salt and pepper
butter for browning

The Sauce
oil for frying
1 onion (finely chopped)
1 red pepper (chopped)
2 cloves garlic (crushed)
250ml chicken stock (see p35)
350g chopped tomatoes
3 cloves
half tsp. cinnamon
1 Chile Guajillo or Serrano

Stuffing
1 hard-boiled egg (chopped)
6 rashers bacon (cooked crisp and chopped)
2 chicken livers (sautéed and chopped)
4 potatoes (boiled and mashed)
handful of parsley (chopped)
salt and pepper

Garnish
lettuce leaves
radish flowers (see p28)

The Sauce
Lightly sauté the chopped vegetables until soft, add the chicken stock, tomatoes, spices and Chile. Simmer for 20 minutes. Blend the sauce.

Flatten the pork fillets into thin sheets of meat. This is done by butterflying the fillets within a centimetre of cutting it in half and gently flatten with a meat hammer. Or ask your butcher. Season with salt and pepper and achiote seasoning. Prepare all the stuffing ingredients and mix well together. Spread a layer of stuffing over the surface of the flattened pork and roll up (Swiss Roll style) securing the flap with toothpicks. Lightly brown the rolled pork by sautéeing in butter. Place in a casserole dish, add sauce and bake in a medium oven 180°C for 20-25 minutes. Place on a serving dish, garnished with lettuce leafs and radish flowers.

Serves 6-8

CHICKEN

- Sister Alberta's Soul Fried Chicken — page 88
- Chicken Stew With Blackeyed Peas and Cornmeal Dumplings — page 89
- Troy's Home Baked Chicken Pie — page 90
- Almond Chicken - Mexican Style (Pollo Almendras - Oaxaca) — page 91
- Chicken In Nut Sauce (Pollos en Nogada - Oaxaca) — page 92
- Yucatan Style Chicken (Pollo Pibil) — page 93
- Table Cloth Stainers (Mancha Mantels) — page 94
- Don Alfredo Chicken (Pollo Don Alfredo) — page 95
- Chicken in Red Wine (Pollo en Vino Tinto) — page 96
- Swiss Enchiladas (Enchiladas Suizas) — page 97
- Chicken in Pumpkin Seed Sauce (Pollo Verde) — page 98
- Chicken Tamale Pie — page 99
- Chicken Jambalaya — page 100
- Chicken in Cream Sauce with Pecans — page 100

SISTER ALBERTA'S SOUL FRIED CHICKEN

2kg chicken
1 tsp. each onion salt, cayenne pepper, mustard powder
flour
salt and pepper
oil for shallow frying

The Gravy
oil and crispy bits from the frying process
25g flour
350ml chicken stock (see p35)
more seasoning if required
small carton single cream (if you really don't care)

Cut up the chicken into pieces, each breast section into 3, drumsticks in two and the remaining leg into three. Trim the wing tips. Place all the dry ingredients in a paper bag along with the chicken pieces and shake until all the chicken is well coated. Remove the chicken from the bag and shake off excess flour. Heat the oil in a large frying pan until very hot but not smoking, and carefully lower each piece of chicken into the oil using tongs. Don't put too many pieces in at once as they should be easily turned. Fry for five minutes then turn each piece, fry for another five minutes then turn again. Fry for a further five minutes and turn again, reduce the heat and fry each side for a final five minutes. The end result should be golden brown fried chicken, crisp on the outside and tender and juicy on the inside. If it browns too quickly the oil is too hot, so reduce the heat. Remove the chicken, drain on kitchen towel and keep it warm in the oven.

To make the gravy, carefully strain the oil (it will be very hot) leaving the crispy bits in the pan with 3 tbsps. of oil. Add the flour and keep stirring to form a light roux. This should take about 10 minutes on a very low heat, stirring constantly. Slowly add the chicken stock, stirring to form gravy. Adjust the seasoning and stir in the cream. Serve over the fried chicken with coleslaw, mashed potatoes and cornbread.

Variation: Add creole sauce (see p37) to the fried chicken and bake for 15 minutes to make an excellent Chicken Creole.
For Country Captain, add curry sauce from the Shrimp Curry (see p62) to the fried chicken.

Serves 4-6

CHICKEN STEW WITH BLACKEYED PEAS AND CORNMEAL DUMPLINGS

Cornmeal Dumplings
300g plain flour
100g cornmeal
4tsp. baking powder
100g butter
100ml milk
2 tbsp. finely chopped parsley
salt and pepper to taste

Chicken Stew
2kg chicken (cut into serving pieces)
2 stalks celery (roughly chopped)
2 carrots (roughly chopped)
salt and pepper
2 bay leaves

250ml milk
2 tsps. cornflour (dissolved in a little milk)
pinch of sage
2 sprigs thyme
Louisiana Hot Sauce
250g dried black-eyed peas (soak and cook until tender)

To make the dumplings sift the dry ingredients, then rub in the butter with your fingers until the mixture resembles breadcrumbs. Stir in the milk, parsley and seasoning and mix to form thick dough. Form into dumplings. Makes approximately 8 small dumplings.

Place the chicken pieces, vegetables and seasonings in a large pot, cover with water and simmer until tender - about an hour. Remove the chicken pieces, strain the stock, and discard the vegetables. Skim the chicken grease from the stock, simmer the strained stock, and add milk. Thicken by slowly pouring in the cornflour mixture. Add sage, thyme, Louisiana Hot Sauce and cooked black-eyed peas. Simmer for 15 minutes to produce a thick gravy. Re-introduce the chicken pieces to the pot and spoon on the dumplings. Simmer covered for 15 minutes to steam the dumplings. Serve chicken with the black-eyed peas spooned over and a dumpling or two on the side.

Great served with Dirty Rice (see p108).
Serves 6

TROY'S HOME BAKED CHICKEN PIE

Troy rang our doorbell at any hour of the day, usually before sunrise and always drugged up to the eyeballs. In 1993 Troy went to bed with a woman and a gun. The whole neighbourhood heard the gunshot. Troy had a hole in his head, and the woman ran screaming from the house. He survived and regained his speech years later but could never remember the events that led to his tragic accident.

2kg chicken (follow Caldo de Pollo recipe see p35, remove the cooked chicken from the bone in big chunks)

25g butter
4 spring onions (chopped)
1 green pepper (chopped)
200g mushrooms (chopped)

50g butter
30g plain flour

250ml chicken stock (see p35)
200g can pimientos (chopped)
100ml milk
salt and pepper to taste

batch of Cornbread Batter (see p112)

Place chunks of chicken in a casserole dish. Melt 25g butter in a frying pan and cook the spring onions, pepper and mushrooms until soft.

Make a light roux with the butter and flour, and add the cooked vegetables. Slowly stir in the chicken stock and simmer for 10 minutes. Add the pimientos, stir in the milk and season with salt and pepper. Pour the creamy vegetable sauce over the cooked chicken, place in a casserole, top with the Cornbread Batter and bake for 25 minutes at 200°C, until the Cornbread is golden brown and cooked.

Serve with your favourite side dish.

Serves 4-6

ALMOND CHICKEN - MEXICAN STYLE
POLLO ALMENDRAS - OAXACA

4 chicken fillets (flatten with a meat hammer and season with salt and pepper)
150g roasted almonds (ground)
butter for frying

50ml single cream

Garnish
25g chopped almonds
coriander leaves

The Sauce
4 dried Chile Pasilla (pulp removed see p28 - 29)
2 hard-boiled egg yolks
1 tsp. cider vinegar
1 tsp. muscovado sugar
qtr. tsp. ground allspice
300ml chicken stock

The Sauce
Blend Chile flesh with the vinegar, egg yolks, sugar and allspice to form a paste. Add chicken stock to the paste a little at a time, blending well after each addition. Simmer in a saucepan, whisking if it requires further blending.

Heat the butter in a frying pan, add the chicken and brown on both sides. Add the ground almonds and continue cooking them together, roasting the almonds further. Pour the Pasilla sauce over chicken and almonds, and simmer chicken in the sauce for 10 minutes until cooked. In the last seconds of cooking, stir in the single cream to thicken the sauce.
Serve immediately garnished with chopped almonds and a sprinkling of coriander leaves.

Serve with rice.

Serves 4

CHICKEN IN NUT SAUCE
POLLOS EN NOGADA - OAXACA

Chicken
4 chicken fillets
25g butter for frying
2 cloves garlic (crushed)
salt & pepper to taste

The Sauce
25g butter
1 medium onion (chopped)
2 cloves garlic (chopped)
50g peanuts (ground)
50g walnuts (ground)
50g French bread toasted and pounded into breadcrumbs
300ml chicken stock (see p35)
2 dried Chile Guajillo (pulp removed see p28 - 29)
1 dried Chile Ancho (pulp removed see p28 - 29)
pinch of ground cinnamon
25g raisins
1 tbsp. crème fraiche

Garnish
25g chopped walnuts
some coriander leaves

The Sauce
Fry the onions and garlic in butter until soft. Add ground nuts and breadcrumbs, and fry for a few minutes, stirring constantly. Add the chicken stock, Chile pulp, cinnamon and raisins. Simmer for 15 minutes to reduce the sauce. Blend the sauce with a hand held blender, stir in the Crème fraiche and set aside.

Chicken
Melt the butter in a frying pan and add the garlic to make garlic butter. Add the chicken and fry until golden brown on both sides. Pour the sauce over the chicken and simmer for five minutes to combine. Lift the chicken out onto plates and pour over sauce. Garnish with chopped walnuts and coriander leaves.
Serve with rice

Serves 4

YUCATAN STYLE CHICKEN
POLLO PIBIL

2kg chicken cut into serving size pieces
4 cloves garlic
2 tbsp. ground annato
qtr. tsp. ground cinnamon
8 cloves
half tsp. black pepper
2 Chile Chipotle (canned in adobo sauce, 2 chiles plus 2 tsp. adobo sauce)
juice from half a pink grapefruit
juice from an orange
1 tbsp. cider vinegar

The Sauce
1 cup water
the pan juices
50g sour cream or crème fraiche

Blend together the spices and garlic. Add the Chile Chipotles and adobo sauce, the juice from the fruits, vinegar and blend into a paste. Rub this paste all over the chicken and marinate for at least 4 hours, preferably overnight. Wrap the chicken pieces in tin foil or banana leaves (if available). Place wrapped chicken on a roasting rack in a tray with 1 cup of water, to catch the juices. Bake slowly for 2 & half hours at 160°C. Remove from the oven, unwrap chicken and shred the meat off the bone. Serve on a platter with plenty of black beans and pickled onions and tortillas. Let everyone make his or her own tacos.

To make the sauce, reduce the juices from the chicken in a saucepan and stir in the sour cream. Place in a bowl to be spooned over the chicken in the tacos.

Serves 4-6

TWO COOKS AND A SUITCASE

TABLECLOTH STAINERS
MANCHA MANTELS

(named after the sauce's ability to ruin the finest tablecloth)

4 chicken breast fillets (cut into cubes)
50g butter
2 courgettes (cubed)
1 plantain (diced)

oil for frying
2 small onions (finely chopped)
4 cloves garlic (crushed)
100g bacon pieces
1kg fresh tomatoes (roasted, skinned and sieved)
250ml chicken stock (see p35)
2 Chile Anchos (soaked and pulp removed)
2 Chile Pasillas (soaked and pulp removed)
2 Chile Chipotles in adobo Sauce (chopped)
salt and pepper to taste

200g fresh pineapple (tinned cubed pineapple may be substituted)

In a little oil, fry the onion and garlic until soft. Add the bacon pieces and fry until cooked. Add the tomatoes, chicken stock, prepared chiles, salt and pepper. Simmer the sauce for 15 minutes, place in a blender and blend until smooth. Add the pineapple and set aside. Meanwhile, fry the chicken in a little butter until golden brown, add the courgettes and plantain and fry until cooked. Pour over the sauce and simmer for 15 minutes.

Serve with rice, preferably on a table with no tablecloth or with a dark brown one.

Serves 4

DON ALFREDO'S CHICKEN
POLLO DON ALFREDO

4 chicken fillets (seasoned)
50g butter

The Sauce
oil for frying
1 medium onion
2 cloves garlic
100g bacon pieces
250ml chicken stock
400g fresh or frozen garden peas
1 Chile Serrano (chopped)
half glass of sherry
salt & pepper to taste

Garnish
4 slices boiled ham (cut into strips)
2 hard-boiled eggs (finely chopped)
2 canned pimientos (cut into long strips)
French bread cut into cubes and fried into croutons
a small bunch of parsley (chopped)

For the sauce, fry the onions and garlic in a little oil, until lightly caramelised, then add the bacon and fry for a further 2 minutes. Add the remaining ingredients and simmer for 15 minutes. In a food processor blend the sauce to a bright green purée, and season with salt and pepper. Fry the chicken in the butter until golden brown on both sides. Pour over the sauce and cook, stirring and turning the chicken for 5 minutes. Place chicken on individual plates or a serving platter. Pour over the sauce and garnish elaborately. Start by sprinkling with chopped boiled eggs, then dot with French bread croutons, then alternate a strip of pimento and a strip of boiled ham. Finish by sprinkling with parsley.

Serves 4

CHICKEN IN RED WINE
POLLO EN VINO TINTO

2kg chicken cut into pieces

100g bacon (finely chopped)
2 dried Chile guajillo (soaked and pulp removed see p28)
1 medium onion (chopped)
4 cloves garlic (crushed)
1 carrot (chopped)
1 glass red wine
250ml chicken stock
1 tsp. cumin
1 tsp. Mexican oregano
half kilo tomatoes (roasted, skinned and sieved)
2 Chile Jalapeno (chopped)
salt and pepper to taste

Boil the chicken as if you are making Caldo de Pollo. Keep some stock for this recipe and freeze the rest. Remove the chicken pieces to a casserole dish. To make the sauce, fry the bacon in a little oil, add the onions, carrot and garlic and cook until soft. Then stir in the wine, stock, spices, Chiles and tomatoes. Simmer the sauce on a low heat for 15 minutes, stirring occasionally to prevent sticking. Pour the sauce over the chicken pieces and bake in a preheated oven at 190°C for 35 minutes. The sauce should be thick and the chicken by this stage should be falling off the bone.

Serve with Mexican Rice (see p120)

Serves 4-6

SWISS ENCHILADAS
ENCHILADAS SUIZAS

1 batch of home made corn tortillas (see p 31) or ready made.
1 batch of Carnitas De Pollo (see p 35)
100g sour cream
200g Monterey Jack cheese

Salsa Verde
oil for frying
4 cloves garlic (chopped)
2 medium onions (chopped)
1 carrot (grated)
1 tsp. sugar
300 ml chicken stock (see p35)
300g fresh or canned tomatillos
2 pickled or fresh Chile Serrano (chopped)
4 tomatoes, roasted, peeled and sieved (see page 29)
1 small handful fresh coriander (finely chopped)
salt & pepper to taste

Salsa Verde
Fry onion and garlic in a little oil until onions have slightly caramelised. Add carrot and sugar and keep frying until carrots have softened. Add the rest of the ingredients and simmer for 20 minutes to blend flavours. Season to taste, adding more chiles if desired. Blend sauce to a smooth consistency.

Dip each tortilla in the Salsa Verde to moisten, fill with Carnitas de Pollo mixture and roll up to form a taco, shaking off excess sauce. Shallow fry the filled tortillas joint sides down to seal them shut, then turn to fry all over. Be careful of splashing oil. When all the tacos are fried, place in a warmed oven dish, smother with Salsa Verde, drizzle with sour cream, sprinkle with cheese and grill until cheese is brown and bubbling. Serve immediately.

Serves 6

CHILAQUILES (a variation of Enchiladas Suizas)

Cut the tortillas into strips and fry until crisp, sprinkle with the shredded Carnitas de Pollo, spoon on the Salsa Verde, drizzle with sour cream, sprinkle with cheese and grill for 5 minutes until cheese melts.

CHICKEN IN PUMPKIN SEED SAUCE
POLLO VERDE

4 chicken fillets (cut into cubes)

150g pumpkin seeds
400g fresh or canned tomatillos
4 spring onions (finely chopped)
2 Chile Serranos (chopped)
200ml chicken stock (see p35)

100g bacon (finely chopped)
3 cloves garlic (crushed)
Oil or butter for frying
150g peanut butter
a handful fresh coriander (chopped)
1 hard-boiled egg (chopped)
some fresh coriander (finely chopped)

Toast the pumpkinseeds in a dry frying pan until they start popping and look roasted. Grind them in a food processor, add the tomatillos, onions, Chiles and chicken stock and blend well. Fry the chicken, bacon and garlic in oil or butter until chicken is golden brown. Pour the pumpkin/tomatillo mixture over the chicken, stir well and simmer together for 15 minutes to blend flavours and cook the chicken. Stir in the peanut butter until it dissolves into the sauce, then stir in the coriander, salt and pepper to taste. Serve over rice garnish with chopped egg and some more coriander.

Serves 4

TWO COOKS AND A SUITCASE

CHICKEN TAMALE PIE

Tamale Dough
200g white Masa Harina
half tsp. baking powder
100g butter (melted)
250ml chicken stock (see p35)
salt and pepper

Filling
1 batch Pollo Verde (see previous recipe)

Red Sauce
1 medium onion
3 cloves garlic (crushed)
250ml chicken stock
6 tomatoes (roasted, skinned and sieved)
half Chile Habanero (use as much as you can stand or just use Habanero hot sauce)
3 sprigs epazote
6 allspice berries
half tsp. Mexican oregano
oil for frying

Garnish
sour cream
fresh coriander

Mix the Masa Harina with the baking powder, then stir in the melted butter and chicken stock to form a dough, slightly thicker than cake mix but not as thick as bread dough. Line a well-greased casserole dish with the dough, spreading it evenly up the sides and over the bottom of the dish. Pour in the Pollo Verde filling and spread the rest of the dough over the top. The filling should be completely enclosed in tamale dough. Bake the pie in the oven at 190°C for 35 minutes or until the top is golden brown. Meanwhile make the Red Sauce. Fry the onion and garlic in a little oil until soft, add the rest of the ingredients and simmer for 15 minutes to produce a thick red sauce.

Place slices of the pie on individual plates and top with Red Sauce, sour cream and some chopped coriander. Serve with rice and refried beans.

Serves 4-6

CHICKEN JAMBALAYA

2kg chicken
40g butter
200g cooked ham
4 cloves garlic (crushed)
4 spring onions (chopped)
1 stalk celery (finely chopped)
2 medium green peppers (chopped)
half tsp. thyme
half tsp. paprika
half tsp. basil

1 can chopped tomatoes
500ml chicken stock (see p35)
1 tbsp. Worcester sauce
some hot sauce (to taste)
salt and pepper to taste
200g long grain rice

Garnish
parsley (chopped)

Boil the chicken in a large pot until tender - about an hour. Once tender, remove the meat from the bone, set aside and reserve the stock.
Heat the butter in a large skillet or frying pan. Sauté the ham and all the vegetables, except the tomatoes, until tender. When tender add the tomatoes and spices. Pour in the chicken stock, Worcester sauce, hot sauce, salt and pepper. Stir in the rice and chicken, cover and continue simmering on a very low heat for 15-20 minutes, until the rice is cooked and all the liquid is gone. Fluff up the rice and garnish with parsley. **Serves 6**

CHICKEN IN CREAM SAUCE WITH PECANS

4 chicken breasts
2 cloves garlic (crushed)
50g butter for frying
250ml chicken stock (see p35)
1 glass white wine
salt and pepper
cayenne pepper

100g chopped pecans
50g butter
142ml double cream

Garnish
some sprigs of parsley
halved pecans

Melt the butter, add the garlic, then fry the chicken in the garlic butter until golden brown on both sides. Pour in the chicken stock and white wine, season with salt, pepper and a little cayenne pepper and simmer for 5 minutes. Remove the chicken and keep it warm in the oven. Simmer the sauce until reduced - about 5 minutes.
Meanwhile, in a small frying pan sauté the chopped pecans in the butter. Add to the reduced sauce, quickly stir in the cream and remove from heat. Do not boil the cream or it will curdle. Remove the chicken from the oven to a serving platter and pour over the sauce. Garnish with a few parsley sprigs and some halved pecans. Serve with rice or potatoes and a vegetable dish. **Serves 4**

CAJUN SIDE DISHES

- Scalloped Potatoes and Mushrooms — *page 102*
- Cream Cheese Potato Casserole — *page 102*
- Potato Loaf — *page 103*
- Stuffed Baked Potatoes - New Orleans Style — *page 103*
- Keller's Cajun Potato Salad — *page 104*
- Sweet Potatoes — *page 104*
- Sweet Potato Balls — *page 105*
- Mushrooms Stuffed With Broccoli — *page 105*
- Corn Stuffed Tomatoes — *page 106*
- Lima Beans and Lentils — *page 106*
- Okra And Tomatoes — *page 107*
- Sufferin' Succotash — *page 107*
- String Bean Salad — *page 108*
- Mr Keller's Cajun Dirty Rice — *page 108*
- Hoppin' John (Black-eyed Peas and Rice) — *page 109*
- Red Beans And Rice — *page 110*
- Soul Baked Macaroni — *page 111*
- Hush Puppies — *page 111*
- Cheese And Jalapeno Cornbread — *page 112*
- Deep Fried Crispy Okra — *page 112*

SCALLOPED POTATO AND MUSHROOM

295g can condensed mushroom soup
500ml milk
2kg potatoes or 6 medium sized (peeled and sliced very thin)
2 onions (sliced)
50g butter (melted)
sprinkling of cayenne pepper
salt and pepper to taste

Whisk together the soup and milk in a bowl. Grease a large casserole dish, place a layer of sliced potato and then a layer of onion, drizzle with the melted butter and then some soup mix. Layer like this until all the ingredients are finished and top with a sprinkling of cayenne pepper. Bake in 170°C oven until the milk has been absorbed, the potatoes are tender and a crust has formed on top - about one hour.

Variation: for traditional Scalloped Potatoes replace the soup with 250ml single cream.
For Scalloped Potatoes Au Gratin top traditional recipe with grated cheese in the last 15 minutes of baking.

Serves 6

CREAM CHEESE POTATO CASSEROLE

2 kg or 6 medium sized potatoes
25g butter
50ml milk
400g cream cheese with chives
2 eggs beaten with 50g flour

1 large onion (chopped)
50g butter
4 dashes Louisiana Hot Sauce

Boil the potatoes in their skin until soft. Cool and peel. Mash the potatoes with the butter and milk, mix thoroughly with the cream cheese, add the beaten egg and flour and mix well. Turn mixture into a greased casserole dish. Caramelise the onions by slowly cooking in the butter, stirring constantly until brown - 15-20 minutes. Shake in some hot sauce and stir. Top the potatoes with the spicy onions. Bake for 30 minutes at 190°C. The potatoes will puff up and brown on top.

Serves 4-6

POTATO LOAF

2kg or 6 medium sized potatoes (peeled and sliced)
4 tbsp. butter
3 tbsp. plain flour
550ml milk
1tsp. cayenne pepper
salt and pepper to taste
1 onion (finely chopped)
1 green pepper (finely chopped)
1 tblsp. fresh parsley (finely chopped)
2 eggs (beaten)

Boil the potatoes until cooked.
Melt the butter in a frying pan, add the flour and blend on a low heat. Slowly pour in the milk, a little at a time, stirring constantly to form a smooth white sauce. To the sauce add salt, pepper, cayenne pepper, onion, green pepper and parsley. Simmer and stir to avoid burning. Pour the sauce over the cooked potatoes and stir in the beaten eggs until thoroughly mixed. Place the mixture in a greased loaf dish and chill overnight. Turn the loaf onto a greased baking sheet and bake in a preheated oven at 175°C for 45 minutes. Once baked, slice and serve. Alternatively, slice the potato loaf cold, coat in egg and breadcrumbs then shallow fry. **Serves 6**

STUFFED BAKED POTATOES NEW ORLEANS STYLE

4 baking potatoes
8 rashers smoked bacon
6 spring onions (finely chopped)
2 tsp. Parmesan cheese (grated)
100g mature Cheddar cheese
3 tbsp. sour cream
salt, pepper and paprika to taste
50g melted butter
2 tbsp. chopped parsley

Bake the potatoes for 1 hour at 180°C until soft. Allow to cool, cut in half and scrape out the insides into a bowl. Set aside. Fry the bacon until crisp, remove from the pan and chop fine. In a little of the bacon grease, sauté the spring onions until lightly browned then add the inside of the potatoes, cheese, sour cream and seasonings. Heat thoroughly on a low heat, stirring constantly to prevent burning. Stuff the potato skins with the mixture then over each half pour a little melted butter and sprinkle with paprika and bacon pieces. Bake in a preheated oven at 175°C for 15-20 minutes until hot. Garnish with parsley. Serve immediately. **Serves 4**

KELLER'S CAJUN POTATO SALAD

2kg or 6 medium sized potatoes
6 eggs
2 stalks celery (finely chopped)
1 green pepper (finely chopped)
3 spring onions (chopped)
340ml mayonnaise
the juice of one lemon
6 tbsp. French dressing
2 tbsp. tomato ketchup
1 tbsp. prepared mustard
salt and pepper to taste

Garnish
half tsp. cayenne pepper
chopped parsley

Peel and chop the potatoes into chunks and boil for 10 minutes until cooked but firm - be careful not to overcook. Hard-boil the eggs. Peel the eggs, remove the egg yolks and chop the egg whites into small pieces. Combine the potato, celery, spring onions, green pepper and egg whites in a large bowl. Squeeze half of the lemon over the potato mixture. To make the dressing, mash the egg yolks with the French dressing, ketchup, mustard, salt, pepper, mayonnaise and the rest of the lemon juice. Stir the dressing into the potato mixture. Form the potato salad into a mound on a serving platter, surround with lettuce and tomato, and garnish with cayenne pepper and finely chopped parsley.

Serves 6-8

SWEET POTATOES

4 sweet potatoes
2 tbsp. brown sugar
75g. butter
1 tsp. nutmeg
1/2 tsp. cinnamon
4 tbsp. water

Put the whole sweet potatoes in boiling water and cook for 20 minutes until tender. Drain the potatoes, cool, then peel and slice them. Place sliced potatoes in a greased casserole dish, dot with the butter, and sprinkle with sugar, nutmeg and cinnamon. Pour over the water to prevent drying up. Bake in a preheated oven at 175°C for 20-25 minutes. **Serves 6**

Cajun Side Dishes

SWEET POTATO BALLS

3 sweet potatoes
75g. butter
salt and pepper to taste
1/4 tsp. nutmeg
small packet peanuts (crushed)

Cook the potatoes as above, scoop out the flesh and mash with butter, salt, pepper and nutmeg. Form the mixture into little balls and roll in crushed peanuts. Place balls on a greased oven tray and bake in a preheated oven at 160°C for 25-30 minutes. Very rich, but very delicious.

Serves 6

MUSHROOMS STUFFED WITH BROCCOLI

8 large or 16 medium mushrooms
6 spring onions (chopped)
2 cloves garlic (crushed)
295g tin condensed cream of celery soup
50g butter
50g good melting cheese (Monterey Jack, Mozzarella or Swiss)
220g broccoli (cooked for 15 minutes, chopped fine)

Remove the stalks from the mushrooms and scrape out a little of the flesh - you can use the stalks for soup or a sauce. Place the mushroom caps on a well-greased oven tray. To make the stuffing, melt the butter in a saucepan, sauté the onions and garlic for 5 minutes then add the celery soup and broccoli and simmer for 15 minutes stirring constantly to prevent sticking. Stuff the mushrooms, sprinkle with grated cheese and bake in a preheated oven at 175°C for 15-20 minutes, until crisp and bubbling on top. Serve immediately.

Serves 4 as a side dish or make a lot for a party

CORN STUFFED TOMATOES

6 large tomatoes hollowed out reserving the inside

Stuffing
1 tbsp. butter
4 spring onions (chopped)
400g of corn kernels
200g tin of pimientos (chopped)
salt and pepper to taste

Melt the butter in a frying pan and sauté the spring onions. Add the corn, pimientos, salt and pepper, and the inside of the tomatoes. Simmer for 15 minutes until all the liquid has gone. Stuff the tomatoes, place on a greased oven dish and bake in a preheated oven at 175°C for 15 minutes.

Serves 6

LIMA BEANS AND LENTILS

200g bacon pieces (chopped)
1 stalk celery (chopped)
4 cloves garlic (chopped)
2 onions (chopped)
1 green pepper (chopped)
400g tin lima beans or Spanish white beans (drained and rinsed)
400g tin Spanish lentils (drained and rinsed)
1 tsp. cayenne pepper
some parsley (chopped)
70g tomato purée
1 tsp. curry powder
1 cup water
salt and pepper to taste

In a little olive oil, briefly sauté the bacon, celery, onion, garlic and green pepper. Stir in the beans, lentils, cayenne, parsley, tomato purée, curry powder and water. Season with salt and pepper and simmer for 10 minutes. Pour mixture into a casserole dish and bake for 25 minutes 170°C.

Serves 6 as a side dish

OKRA AND TOMATOES

450g okra (fresh or frozen)

50g butter
1 onion (chopped)
2 tins chopped tomatoes (900g)
salt to taste
half tsp. black pepper
3 drops Tabasco™ sauce

If using fresh okra, clean thoroughly, cut off the tops and tails and cook in boiling water for 15 minutes over a low-medium heat. If using frozen okra follow the instructions on the packet.

Melt the butter in a frying pan and fry the onion until soft. Add the tomatoes, salt, pepper and Tabasco™. Stir in thoroughly. Add the cooked okra and simmer for 10 minutes. Transfer to a casserole dish and bake in a preheated oven at 175°C for 20 minutes. This dish is also delicious with a topping of grated cheese.

Serves 4-6 as a side dish

SUFFERIN' SUCCOTASH

olive oil for frying
100g minced ham
1 stalk celery (chopped)
2 onions (chopped)
2 cloves garlic (chopped)
1 small green pepper (chopped)
2 x 400g cans Lima beans or Spanish white beans (drained and rinsed)
1x 425g tin sweetcorn
1 carton single cream
1 tsp. sugar
salt and pepper to taste
2 pickled Chile Jalapeno (chopped)

In a little olive oil fry the minced ham and vegetables. Fry for 10 minutes then add the beans and corn, and stir in the cream. Add the sugar, and season with salt, pepper and Jalapeños. Simmer gently for five minutes.

Serves 6 as a side dish

STRING BEAN SALAD

250g string beans (cut in half and boiled until tender)
100g fresh or frozen peas (cooked for a few minutes)
2 spring onions (finely chopped)
2 kosher dill pickles (chopped)
1 small green pepper (chopped)
1 stalk celery (chopped)
2 canned pimientos (sliced)
2 hard-boiled eggs (yolk separated from white)
4 tbsp. mayonnaise
salt and pepper

Place all the prepared vegetables in a salad bowl. Mix the egg yolk with the mayonnaise, and then add the chopped egg white and season with salt and pepper. Fold this into the salad vegetables and chill. Serve on crunchy lettuce leaves. **Serves 6 as a side dish**

MR. KELLER'S CAJUN DIRTY RICE
(traditionally made with chicken gizzards and liver, Mr. Keller don't do offal, so this is his version)

30ml oil for frying
3 onions (chopped)
1 stalk celery (chopped)
1 green pepper (chopped)
2 cloves garlic (chopped)
250g ground pork
350ml chicken stock (see p35)
salt and pepper
pinch of thyme
pinch of oregano
Louisiana Hot Sauce (as much as you like)
250g rice (washed thoroughly)

Sauté the vegetables for 5-10 minutes until soft. Add the ground pork and brown well, mixing the meat through the vegetables. Add the chicken stock, herbs, seasoning and hot sauce, and simmer for another 15 minutes. Add the rice, checking the liquid level - there should be 3cm above the meat and vegetables. Cover and simmer on a very low heat for 20 minutes - no peeking ! Turn off the heat and leave for 5 minutes. Fluff up the rice mixture and serve with your favourite Cajun, Creole or soulfood dishes. Or serve as a supper dish on its own. **Serves 6**

HOPPIN' JOHN
BLACK EYED PEAS AND RICE

Traditionally served on New Year's Day, but good at any time of the year. The name is said to derive from the tradition of hopping round the table three times for good luck, or perhaps unexpected friends turn up hoppin' for some beans and rice - who knows?

500g dried black eyed beans (washed and soaked)
1 ham hock

oil for frying
2 stalks celery (chopped)
4 cloves garlic (minced)
6 spring onion (chopped)
1 large green pepper (chopped)
2 bay leaves
1 handful chopped parsley
1tsp. cayenne pepper
salt and pepper to taste

250g long grain rice (cooked)

Soak the beans overnight, wash thoroughly. Place ham hock and washed beans in a large pot, cover with water, bring to the boil, reduce the heat and simmer for 45 minutes. Then remove the ham hock (keep the beans on a gentle simmer), cool and cut off the meat, returning it to the pot as you do so. Sauté the vegetables in a little oil. When soft add them to the simmering beans along with the bay leaves, cayenne, parsley, salt and pepper. Simmer for 15-20 minutes. Stop now if you want to serve up just black eyed beans. To make Hoppin' John stir in the cooked rice and heat through.

Serves at least 8 with a heap of crusty bread and a bottle of hot sauce. Can also be used as a side dish.

RED BEANS AND RICE

500g dried red beans (picked through and sorted)

1 large ham hock or ham joint
1 green pepper
50g butter
1 large onion
2 stalks celery
1 carrot
4 cloves garlic
2 bay leaves
1 tsp. thyme
1 tsp. sugar
Louisiana Hot Sauce
salt and pepper to taste

250g cooked white rice
chopped parsley garnish

Soak the beans overnight and wash thoroughly. Put beans in a large pot with plenty of water. Bring to the boil, reduce the heat and simmer for 30 minutes. Then add the ham hock and continue simmering.
Meanwhile, sauté vegetables in butter until soft. Add the cooked vegetables, bay leaves, thyme, sugar and hot sauce to the bean pot. Simmer until the beans are tender, adding boiling water as necessary. Season with salt and pepper to taste. Remove the hock or joint and slice or chop up the meat, returning it to the pot for 10 minutes. Serve over rice, garnish with chopped parsley.

This is one of those dishes that always taste better the next day.

Variation: In Caribbean cooking they always add a tin of coconut milk and some curry powder. Chorizo or Creole Sausage makes a great addition.

Serves 6-8 people with some left over for supper

SOUL BAKED MACARONI

This is the stodgy type, not saucy, and brings back memories of every soulfood dive I've ever eaten in. A must with pork chops.

250g elbow macaroni
50g butter
some chopped parsley
hot sauce to taste
salt and pepper to taste
220g sharp Cheddar (grated)
1 can evaporated milk
2 beaten eggs

Boil a large pan of salted water, place the macaroni in and boil until cooked - about 12 minutes. Drain macaroni and rinse in hot water. Transfer macaroni into a large casserole dish. Break off pieces of butter and dot them over the macaroni along with the parsley, salt, pepper and hot sauce. Stir until the butter has melted. Sprinkle on the grated cheese. Beat the eggs in a bowl, beat in the evaporated milk, pour the mixture over the cheese and macaroni, and stir in with a fork. Bake for 40 minutes at 190°C until the top is well browned.

Variations: just in case you don't think this dish is fattening enough, try cooling the Macaroni Cheese, cut into slices, dip the slices in egg and flour and shallow fry to make crisp Macaroni Fritters. Truly soul satisfying. **Serves 4-6**

HUSH PUPPIES

350g cornmeal
150g plain flour
2 tsp. baking powder
1 tsp. salt
4 spring onions
250ml milk
2 eggs
oil for deep-frying

Mix the cornmeal, flour, baking powder, salt and spring onions. Beat the eggs and milk together. Add to the dry ingredients to form a batter, similar in texture to a sponge cake batter. Drop tablespoons of the batter into hot oil and fry until golden brown. Drain on kitchen towel. Serve immediately. Particularly good with fish dishes or gumbo.

"Hush Puppy!" cried the cook as the dogs were thrown some fried cornmeal batter, allowing the process of frying the fish or chicken to continue. Now everyone howls for them. **Serves 4-6 as a side dish**

CHEESE AND JALAPEÑO CORNBREAD

275g cornmeal
150g plain flour
4 tsp. baking powder
salt
50g sugar
100g butter
300ml milk
2 eggs (beaten)
Chile Jalapeno to taste
100g Cheddar (grated)
salt and pepper to taste

Sift the cornmeal, flour, baking powder and salt into a large bowl and stir in the sugar. Melt the butter in a pan, turn off the heat and pour in the milk. Add this milk and butter mix, and the eggs, to the bowl and mix well. Add chopped Jalapeños and cheese and stir gently. Turn the mixture into a greased oven dish and bake at 200°C for 20 minutes or until a toothpick inserted into the centre comes out clean.

Variation: you can leave the Jalapeño out if you don't like heat.
A can of corn kernels or creamed corn can be added for a delicious variation.

Serves 4-6 as a side dish

DEEP FRIED CRISPY OKRA

450g fresh okra
1 egg (beaten)
2 tbsp. water
280ml milk
100g plain flour
100g finely crushed crackers
salt and pepper to taste

Wash and trim the okra and cut into bite size pieces. Mix the egg, water and milk together, place the okra into the liquid and coat, then drain off excess liquid. Mix flour, crackers, salt and pepper together and coat the okra shaking off any excess. In a deep fat fryer cook okra for 2-5 minutes in hot fat until crisp. Drain on a paper towel and serve immediately.

Serves 4-6

Mexican Side Dishes

MEXICAN SIDE DISHES

- Refried Beans (Refritos) — page 114
- Two Marias Pinto Bean Stew (Frijoles de Dos Marias) — page 115
- Lentils with Fruit (Lentejas Con Fruta) — page 116
- Vegetable Platter (Plato Grande de Verduras) — page 117
- Governor's Spaghetti (Spaghetti Gobernador) — page 118
- Stuffed Avocado Omelette (Aguacate Relleno) — page 118
- Gulf of Mexico Salad (Ensalada del Golfo - Progresso) — page 119
- Cactus Salad (Ensalada de Noplitos) — page 119
- Mexican Patatas Brava (Chile Con Papa) — page 120
- White Rice (Arroz Blanco) — page 120
- Green Rice (Arroz Verde) — page 121
- Roasted Pepper Salad — page 121
- Baked Courgettes with Cheese (Calabacitas Con Queso) — page 122
- Motul Style Eggs — page 122
- Eggs from Cafe Friendly (Huevo de Café Frendle) — page 123

REFRIED BEANS
REFRITOS

*500g pinto or black beans
1 ham hock (optional for vegetarians)*

*3 bay leaves
1 tsp. cumin
1 tsp. Mexican oregano
1 onion (chopped)
6 cloves garlic (crushed)
salt and pepper to taste*

vegetable shortening or lard for frying

75g Cheshire or Wensleydale cheese

Soak the beans overnight and wash thoroughly. Bring the beans and ham hock to the boil in plenty of fresh water, reduce the heat and simmer for 45 minutes, adding more water if required. Add the bay leaves, cumin, oregano, onion and garlic. Simmer for a further 20 minutes, add salt and pepper to taste. Remove the ham hock and bay leaves and mash roughly with a potato masher.
Take a large frying pan, melt the lard, spoon in the mashed beans and fry stirring constantly until thoroughly cooked. (The prefix 're-' in Spanish suggests 'thoroughly', not 'done again' as it does in English). Place in a serving dish and sprinkle with crumbled Cheshire or Wensleydale cheese.

Make a big batch of these and freeze in small containers. They can be defrosted and pan-fried easily when you need them.

Serves 4-6

TWO MARIAS PINTO BEAN STEW
FRIJOLES DE DOS MARIAS

500g Spanish white beans (soaked 8 hours then washed thoroughly)

olive oil for frying
2 onions (chopped)
4 cloves garlic (chopped)
2 cooking Chorizo (sliced)
4 tomatoes (roasted, peeled and chopped)
250ml chicken stock (see p35)
1 can sardines in tomato sauce
1tsp. cumin seeds (toasted and ground)
1tsp oregano
salt and pepper
2 Chile Serrano (chopped)

crumbled Wensleydale cheese
guacamole (see p39)
radish flowers (see p28)

Bring the beans to a boil in plenty of water, reduce heat and simmer until the beans are soft - about 45 minutes. Drain and set aside. Meanwhile, heat the olive oil in a pan, sauté the onions and garlic until soft, add the Chorizo and fry until browned. Add the tomatoes, chicken stock, sardines, cumin, oregano, Serrano, salt and pepper. Gently simmer to reduce liquid, for 15 minutes. Add the cooked beans and cook a further 15 minutes, stirring as required. Place on a serving dish, adorn with crumbled Wensleydale cheese, blobs of guacamole and topped with radish flowers.

Serve with Home Fried Tortilla Chips.

Serves 4-6 as a side dish

LENTILS WITH FRUIT
LENTEJAS CON FRUTA

500g lentils (Puy or Spanish green)

oil for frying
2 onions (chopped)
4 cloves garlic (crushed)
150g bacon pieces
250ml chicken stock (see p35)
2-4 Chile Serrano (chopped)
4 tomatoes (roasted, peeled and sieved)
salt and pepper to taste
fresh coriander (chopped)

1 plantain (sliced and fried in butter until golden brown)
2 pears (peeled, cored and chopped)
2 rings of pineapple (chopped)
2 potatoes (peeled, cubed and cooked)

Thoroughly wash the lentils, put in a pot, cover with water and bring to the boil. Reduce heat and simmer for 20 minutes. Drain and place in a casserole dish. Meanwhile, sauté the onions and garlic in a little oil until soft. Stir in the bacon pieces and lightly brown. Add the stock, tomatoes, Chiles, coriander, salt and pepper, and simmer for 10 minutes. Then add the fruit and potatoes, pour into the lentils and bake for 20 minutes 190°C.

Serves 4

TWO COOKS AND A SUITCASE

VEGETABLE PLATTER
PLATO GRANDE DE VERDURAS

2 large potatoes (cubed)
2 carrots (cubed)
1 cauliflower (cut into small florets)
6 bay leaves
olive oil for frying

150g frozen peas (cooked)
420g can of sweetcorn or preferably 2 corn cobs
2 tomatoes (chopped)
2 avocados (chopped)
pickled Chile Serrano (cut into strips or flowers)

Dressing
100ml olive oil
30ml cider vinegar
4 cloves garlic (toasted and minced)
juice of 1 lime
a small handful chopped coriander
a pinch sugar
salt and pepper to taste
Mexican oregano

Boil the potatoes, carrots and cauliflower with the bay leaves until they are cooked but still firm. Remove the cauliflower after 10 minutes and continue cooking the rest for a further 10 minutes. Drain the vegetables and lightly fry in olive oil. Arrange on a salad platter. If using corn on the cob, grill until brown and then slice into thick chunks. Add to the platter, scatter over the peas, tomato and avocado, and decorate with some Chile Serrano. Whisk the dressing ingredienst together and pour over the vegetables. Serve with crisp fried corn tortillas. I recommend serving this while the cooked vegetables are still warm.

Use as a vegetable side dish or to accompany a beer drinking session.

Serves 4-6

GOVERNOR'S SPAGHETTI
SPAGHETTI GOBERNADOR

500g spaghetti (broken up into random sized pieces)

oil for frying
4 spring onions (chopped)
4 cloves garlic (chopped)
250ml chicken stock (see p35)
100g crème fraiche
200g cooked chicken breast
100g bacon (grilled crisp)
1 Chile Poblano or New Mexican (roasted, peeled and chopped)
200g can peas
340ml mayonnaise
1 bunch parsley (chopped)
salt and pepper

Boil the spaghetti in plenty of salted water until cooked, then drain. In a frying pan, sauté the spring onions and garlic until soft, add the chicken stock and crème fraiche, and simmer for a few minutes. Add the cooked chicken, bacon, Chiles and peas. Toss in the cooked spaghetti, season with salt and pepper. Mix through the parsley and mayonnaise. Season and serve warm. **Serves 4-6**

STUFFED AVOCADO OMELETTE
AGUACATE RELLENO

oil for frying
3 Hass avocados (peeled)
1 portion Picadillo (see p78) or cream cheese for a vegetarian option
3 eggs (beaten)
olive oil
salt and pepper

Cut the avocados in half, remove the stone and fill each half with picadillo or cheese. Put a little oil in a non-stick omelette pan, place all the avocados cut side down in the pan, pour over the egg and cook over a low heat until the egg has set. Flip over and brown on the reverse side. Serve with Salsa De Chipotle. (see p40).

The end result should be like an omelette set around stuffed half avocados. Try making individual omelettes in a small pan. **Serves 4-6**

Mexican Side Dishes

GULF OF MEXICO SALAD
ENSALADA DEL GOLFO - PROGRESSO

Salad

1 chicken (cooked and shredded) (Carnitas see p35)
3 carrots (cooked, then diced)
500g potatoes (cooked, then diced)
200g cooked garden peas (canned or fresh)
400g tin roasted red pepper (chopped)
100g pecan nuts (chopped)
salt and pepper to taste
fresh oregano (chopped)
340ml mayonnaise
2 Chile Poblano (roasted and chopped) or 2 canned Poblanos (chopped)
small handful fresh coriander (chopped)

Garnish

lettuce leaves
6 sliced tomatoes
2 hard-boiled eggs (chopped)
radish flowers (see p28)
olives

Put all the salad ingredients in a large bowl and mix thoroughly.
Take a platter and line with lettuce leaves. Load on the chicken salad, surround with sliced tomatoes, sprinkle with chopped boiled egg and garnish with radish flowers and olives. **Serves 6**

CACTUS SALAD
ENSALADA DE NOPALITOS

350g jar nopalitos (cactus) (drained and rinsed)
4 tomatoes (chopped into chunks)
1 red onion (chopped)
3 Chile Jalapeno (chopped)
1 handful fresh coriander (chopped)
Feta cheese (crumbled)

Dressing

juice of 2 limes
4 tbsp. olive oil
3 cloves garlic (roasted, peeled and chopped)
1 Chile Chipotle en adobo (minced)
1 tbsp. red wine vinegar
salt and pepper

Into a big bowl, throw the nopalitos, tomato, onion, chiles and coriander and sprinkle over the crumbled cheese. In a jar mix the olive oil, Chipotle, limejuice, garlic, vinegar, salt and pepper. Shake vigorously to blend. Pour the dressing over the salad and toss. **Serves 4**

MEXICAN PATATAS BRAVAS
CHILE CON PAPA

4 potatoes (peeled, parboiled and diced)
vegetable oil for frying

parsley (chopped)
mature Manchego or Parmesan (finely grated)

Sauce
1 onion (chopped)
2 cloves garlic (chopped)
olive oil for frying
4 tomatoes (roasted, peeled and sieved)
100ml white wine
1 tbsp. pickled sliced Chile Jalapeno

To make the sauce, fry the onions and garlic in the oil until soft, then add the tomatoes, white wine and sliced Jalapeños. Simmer for 15 minutes. Season with salt and pepper.
Take the par-boiled potatoes, slice or dice them, fry in oil until crisp and golden brown, drain on kitchen paper and sprinkle with salt. Just before serving, pour over the Chile Jalapeno sauce and sprinkle with the grated cheese and parsley.

Alternatively you can serve the potatoes with the sauce on the side.

Serves 4

WHITE RICE
ARROZ BLANCO

250g long grain rice (washed)
4 whole cloves garlic
2 tbsp. olive oil
300ml chicken stock (see p35)
salt and pepper

Fry the garlic in the olive oil until golden brown, remove from the oil and add the raw grains of rice to the pan. Stir constantly whilst cooking until the first grains take on a very light brown hue round the edges. Add the chicken stock and seasoning - the stock will splutter when it hits the hot pan. Turn the heat to a low simmer, put a lid on it and cook for 20 minutes - no peeking! Remove from heat and let stand for 5 minutes before fluffing with a fork.

Rice cooking tip: judging the right amount of stock to rice ratio is the secret to perfect rice. I've cooked rice for 2 people and 20 people and my rough judgement, no matter what size the pan, is based on the liquid being 3 cm. above the level of the rice. Make this judgement just before covering the rice.
When cooking Basmati the same rule applies, but when cooking brown rice double the quantity to 6 cm.

Serves 4

GREEN RICE
ARROZ VERDE

2 Chile Poblano (roasted, peeled and de-seeded)
6 tomatillos (chopped)
handful fresh coriander
6 large spinach leaves
300ml chicken stock (see p35)
vegetable oil for frying
250g long grain rice (washed)
2 cloves garlic (roasted)
1 onion (chopped)
1 large corn on the cob (boiled and shucked i.e. kernels removed) or 100g frozen kernels
salt and pepper to taste

In a food processor blend Poblanos, tomatillos, coriander, spinach and chicken stock. Sauté the onion and garlic in oil until soft and add the rice, stirring constantly to coat in oil. Pour the blended ingredients over the rice, add the corn to the pot and season with salt and pepper. When the liquid reaches a simmer put a lid on the pot and cook for 20 minutes on the lowest heat. Turn off the heat and leave to rest for 5 minutes. Fluff and serve.

If you can't get fresh tomatillos or Poblanos then use tinned.

Serves 4

ROASTED PEPPER SALAD

1 red pepper (roasted and skinned)
1 green pepper (roasted and skinned)
1 yellow pepper (roasted and skinned)
2 cloves garlic (minced)
20 pimiento stuffed olives (sliced)
2 tbsp. olive oil
100g Feta (crumbled)

Dressing
4 fresh plum tomatoes (roasted, peeled and sieved)
1 tbsp. fresh oregano
half tsp. cumin (toasted and ground)
2 tsp. cider vinegar
salt and pepper

Slice the roasted peppers into strips and place in a shallow baking dish, alternating the coloured strips. Scatter the sliced olives over the peppers. Mix the dressing ingredients and pour over the peppers. Bake at 180°C for 20 minutes.
Remove from the oven, drizzle with olive oil, sprinkle with Feta and serve warm.

Serves 4

BAKED COURGETTES WITH CHEESE
CALABACITAS CON QUESO

4 courgettes (sliced)
2 eggs (beaten)

Topping
200g crème fraiche
Monterey Jack cheese
home made salsa (see p39)

Seasoned Flour
50g plain flour
50g Masa Harina
salt and pepper
oil for frying

Mix all seasoned flour ingredients together. Dip the courgette slices in egg and coat with the seasoned flour. For an even coating, put the flour in a large paper bag, drop in 6 slices of courgette, and shake.
Shallow fry in batches on a medium heat until golden brown, then drain on kitchen paper.
Place the fried slices in a single layer in an oven proof dish, and sprinkle with salsa, crème fraiche and jack cheese.
Bake in a hot oven for 10 minutes, until the cheese is bubbling. Brown under the grill for a few minutes.

Serves 6

MOTUL STYLE EGGS

6 home made Gorditas de Papa (15cm diameter) (see p55)
a portion Black Refried Beans (see p114)
a portion Chiltomate Sauce (see p38)

butter for frying
3 plantains (cut in half and then split down the middle)
6 eggs (beaten)
100g cooked ham (chopped)
100g frozen or fresh garden peas
salt and pepper to taste

crumbled Feta or Wensleydale cheese

Melt the butter in a pan and cook the plantain until golden. Put aside and keep warm. Add the ham and eggs to the pan with more butter if required. Scramble the egg and ham together. Add the peas.
Take one Gordita per person, spread with black beans, place a piece of plantain on each side of the topped Gordita to form a boat shape, and top with the egg mixture. Garnish with Chiltomate sauce and crumbled cheese.

Serves 6

Mexican Side Dishes

EGG'S FROM CAFE FRIENDLY
HUEVO DE CAFÉ FRENDLE

250ml Caldo De Pollo (see p35)
150g Refried Beans (see p114)
4 tomatoes (roasted, peeled and sieved)
salt and pepper to taste
6 eggs

150g Feta or Cheshire cheese
parsley (chopped)
2 Chile Chipotle en adobo (thinly sliced)

Mix the chicken stock with the refried beans and sieved tomatoes. Blend to form a bean sauce. Season with salt and pepper. Put the bean sauce in an oven dish and carefully break the eggs into the bean sauce. Bake until the eggs are just cooked. Sprinkle with crumbled Cheshire or Feta cheese, parsley and sliced Chile.

Serve with crisp fried tortilla triangles.

Serves 6

DESSERTS

- Pastries for Southern Pies — *page 125*
- Classic Pecan Pie — *page 126*
- Pumpkin Pie — *page 126*
- Cinnamon Cheesecake — *page 127*
- Cheesecake with Caramel Pecan Topping — *page 128*
- Strawberry Cheesecake — *page 129*
- Lemon And Orange Chiffon Pie — *page 130*
- Chocolate Lime Meringue Pie — *page 131*
- Banana Cream Pie — *page 132*
- Flaming Bananas — *page 132*
- Pina Colada Tamales — *page 133*
- Mississippi Mud Cake — *page 134*

PASTRIES FOR SOUTHERN PIES

These pastries will be asked for in some of the following dessert recipes. They are for single 9-inch piecrusts.

SHORTCRUST PASTRY

240g plain flour
qtr. tsp. salt
120g butter
2-3 tblsps. cold water

Sift the flour and salt together into a bowl. Chop the butter into little pieces and add to the flour. Blend with your fingers until mixture resembles fine breadcrumbs. Add 2 tblsp. water and mix. If you can form into a dough then don't add anymore water (too much water will make the dough tough). If you need to add more water just add a little at a time and mix well until mixture forms into dough. Form dough into a ball, wrap in cling film and refrigerate for one hour before using.

SWEET SHORTCRUST PASTRY

120g butter
50g sugar
1 egg
qtr. tsp. salt
240g plain flour

In a food processor, cream the butter and sugar together with the metal blade. Add the egg and pulse until well combined. Pour in the flour and salt and pulse until the dough is formed. Remove from the bowl, wrap in cling film and refrigerate for one hour before using.

CLASSIC PECAN PIE

1 recipe Shortcrust Pastry (see p125)

4 eggs
75g light muscovado sugar
150ml maple syrup
150ml Karo corn syrup
25g melted butter
1 tsp. vanilla extract
80g pecans

Grease a 9-inch pie dish, roll out the pastry and fit into the pan. Preheat oven to 200°C, gas mark 5.

Beat the eggs until light, add the sugar and syrups and beat until well blended. Stir in the melted butter and vanilla extract. Spread the pecans evenly over the bottom of the pastry. Pour the egg mixture over the nuts and bake in the oven for 30-35 minutes or until cooked in the centre. Serve hot or cold with cream or ice cream. **Serves 8**

PUMPKIN PIE

1 recipe Shortcrust Pastry (see p125)

1 can pumpkin
3 eggs
100g dark muscovado sugar
2 tbsps. plain flour
3 tbsps. maple syrup
qtr. tsp. ground cloves
qtr. tsp. ground cinnamon
qtr. tsp. ground ginger
120ml evaporated milk
1 tsp. vanilla extract

Grease a 9-inch pie dish and line with the shortcrust pastry.

Beat the eggs in a large bowl with an electric mixer, add the sugar and beat until well combined. Add the rest of the ingredients and beat until well combined. Pour the mixture into the pastry and bake in a preheated oven at 200°C, gas mark 5 for 50 minutes. Serve hot or cold with whipped cream or vanilla ice cream.

Variations: if desired you can stir in 80g pecan nuts after all the ingredients have been mixed together. Or you can stir in 2 tblsp. of Bourbon at the end to give it that extra kick. **Serves 8**

CINNAMON CHEESECAKE

Base
250g digestive biscuits
25g sugar
75g butter

Filling
600g cream cheese
100g muscovado sugar
qtr. tsp. salt
3 large eggs
3 tsp. ground cinnamon
1 tsp. vanilla extract
140mls sour cream

Butterscotch Sauce
60g brown sugar
25g butter
1 tbsp. Karo corn syrup
40mls water

Grease a 9-inch springform pan.

Crush the biscuits and mix with the sugar. Melt the butter and fold into the biscuits until well combined. Spread evenly over the bottom of the greased pan and flatten with the back of a spoon. Chill in the fridge.

In a food processor cream the cheese until light. Add the sugar, salt and cinnamon and pulse until well blended. Add the eggs one at a time, beating well after each addition. Pour into a bowl and stir in the vanilla extract and sour cream. Pour mixture into the pastry and bake in a preheated oven at 180°C gas mark 4 for 50-60 minutes. The cake should be a little wobbly in the middle. This will cook as it cools. Let the cheesecake cool and remove from pan.

To make the sauce, place the sugar butter and syrup in a saucepan and gently heat, stirring constantly until the sugar has dissolved. Bring to the boil and let bubble for a few minutes. Add the water and keep stirring until well combined, cool to thicken. Drizzle over individual slices of Cinnamon Cheesecake.

Serves 8-10

CHEESECAKE WITH CARAMEL PECAN TOPPING

Topping
1 small tin condensed milk
80g pecans (toasted)

Base
300g plain chocolate digestive
80g butter.

Cheesecake
800g cream cheese
200g sugar
qtr. tsp. salt
4 large eggs
220g sour cream
1 tsp. vanilla extract
1 tbsp. lemon juice

Grease a 10-inch spring form pan, sides and bottom.

Boil the unopened tin of condensed milk in a pan for two hours. Leave to cool completely before opening.

Crush the biscuits in a food processor or in a bowl with a rolling pin. Melt the butter and mix thoroughly with the crushed biscuits. Pour into the greased pan, spread evenly over the bottom and flatten with the back of a spoon. Place in the fridge.

In a food processor beat the cheese and sugar together. Add salt, vanilla and lemon juice and beat until well combined. Add the eggs one at a time, beating well after each addition. Pour mixture into a bowl and stir in the sour cream. Pour mixture onto the biscuit base and place in a preheated oven at 180°C gas mark 4 for 60-70 minutes. Remove from the oven. Don't let the cheesecake cook all the way through, leave it a little wobbly in the middle as it keeps on cooking. Let the cheesecake cool completely, then chill in the fridge for 2 hours. Once chilled, open the can of condensed milk, empty into a bowl and stir in the pecans. Spread mixture over the top of the cheesecake.

Serves 10-12

STRAWBERRY CHEESECAKE

Filling
1 sachet gelatin
6 tbsp. water
3 eggs separated
120g caster sugar
60mls single cream
400g cream cheese
2 tsp. finely shredded lemon peel
1 tbsp. lemon juice
1 tsp. vanilla extract
140mls whipping cream

Base
250g Oreo cookies
75g butter

Topping
300g strawberries/200mls juice
100g caster sugar
1 tbsp. cornflour
4 tbsps. water

Grease a 9-inch springform pan.

Crush the Oreos to make fine crumbs. Melt the butter and mix with the cookies. Pour into the greased pan, spread evenly over the bottom and flatten with the back of a spoon. Place in the fridge.

Sprinkle the gelatin over the water to soften. In a saucepan place the egg yolks, sugar and cream and heat gently, stirring constantly until the mixture thickens. Remove from heat. In a saucepan gently heat the gelatin mix, stirring until completely dissolved, then quickly put through a strainer into the egg yolk mix and stir until thoroughly mixed. Set aside and let cool. Meanwhile, in a food processor, beat the cheese until smooth. Add the lemon peel, juice and vanilla extract and beat until well combined. Whip the cream. Gently fold the cheese mixture and cream into the egg yolks/gelatin mix until well combined - this will take a while. Finally beat the egg whites until stiff and gently fold into the cheesecake mix. Pour onto the biscuit base and refrigerate for at least 2 hours until set.

For the topping, if you have a juicer, put the strawberries through it and use the juice. This should yield about 200mls juice. If not, crush the strawberries and pass through a strainer to get rid of all the seeds. Put the sugar and cornflour in a saucepan and stir in the strawberry juice and water. Heat over a medium heat stirring constantly until boiling. Remove from heat and set aside to cool. Once cooled spread over the top of the set cheesecake, return to the fridge and leave in the pan until set.

Serves 8

LEMON AND ORANGE CHIFFON PIE

Base
250g chocolate digestive biscuits
75g butter

Filling
4 eggs separated
240g sugar
1 sachet gelatin
100mls strained lemon juice (fresh)
100mls strained orange juice (fresh)
qtr. tsp. salt
half tsp. grated lemon peel
half tsp. grated orange peel
140 mls. whipping cream

Grease a 9-inch springform pan.

Crush the biscuits to fine crumbs. Melt the butter and mix thoroughly with the biscuit crumbs. Turn into the greased pan, spread evenly over the bottom and flatten with the back of a spoon. Place in the fridge.

Sprinkle the gelatin over the orange juice to soften. Beat the egg yolks and pour into a saucepan. Add 120g of the sugar, lemon juice, orange juice/gelatin and salt. Cook over a low heat, stirring constantly until the gelatin is dissolved and the mixture begins to thicken -about 10 minutes. Remove from heat and stir in the orange and lemon peel. Set aside to cool. Meanwhile, beat the egg whites until soft peaks appear, then gradually beat in the remaining 120g sugar a little at a time until stiff peaks form. Whip the cream. Gradually fold the egg whites and whipped cream into the gelatin mixture until well combined. Turn mixture onto the biscuit base and refrigerate for at least 2 hours until set.

Serves 8

CHOCOLATE LIME MERINGUE PIE

Crust
1 recipe Sweet Shortcrust Pastry (see p125)
this will make slightly more pastry than you need.

Filling
140g sugar
3 tbsps. cornflour
160ml water
3 egg yolks
80ml strained lime juice (fresh)
100g plain chocolate (70% cocoa solids)
20g butter

Meringue
3 egg whites
pinch of salt
140g caster sugar

Grease an 8" loose bottomed flan tin. Roll out pastry and line the bottom and sides of the tin with this. Prick the pastry with a fork all over the base. Bake blind in a preheated oven at 200°C gas mark 5 for 10-15 minutes until cooked.

Melt the chocolate and butter together and set aside to cool. Meanwhile in a saucepan blend the sugar and cornflour, and gradually stir in the water. Stir in the egg yolks and limejuice. Cook, stirring constantly, over a low heat until mixture thickens. Remove from heat and stir in melted chocolate. Turn into the pastry shell. Let cool.

For the meringue, beat the egg whites with a pinch of salt until stiff peaks appear. Gradually fold in the sugar. Spread over the pie and bake in a preheated oven at 150°C gas mark 3 for 20 minutes until lightly browned on top. Cool completely and serve.

Serves 6-8

BANANA CREAM PIE

4 bananas
freshly squeezed lemon juice
qtr. tsp. nutmeg
qtr. tsp. cinnamon

Base
250g ginger nuts
75g butter

Filling
1 sachet gelatin
125ml water
125ml milk
6 egg yolks
150g sugar
1 tsp. vanilla extract
140mls whipping cream

Grease a 9-inch springform pan.

Cut bananas in half lengthways. Mix the lemon juice, nutmeg and cinnamon together and pour over the bananas. Bake in a preheated oven at 200°C gas mark 5 for 10 minutes. Remove from oven and set aside to cool.
For the base, crush the ginger nuts, melt the butter and stir into the biscuits until well combined. Turn into the pan and flatten with the back of a spoon evenly over the bottom. Chill in the fridge.

For the filling mix the gelatin and milk over a low heat until the gelatin dissolves - about 10 minutes. Remove from stove to cool slightly. Cream sugar and egg yolks together, stir a little of the milk into the eggs and then pour the eggs into the milk and return to the stove. Cook over a low heat stirring constantly for 15-20 minutes. Remove from the stove and stir in the vanilla extract. Set aside to cool. Whip the cream and gently fold into the egg mixture. Pour over the base and chill in the fridge until set - about two hours.

Serves 8

FLAMING BANANAS

6 bananas
125g butter
120g muscovado sugar
2 tbsps. Cointreau
2 tbsps. rum
6 scoops vanilla ice cream

Melt the butter in a large frying pan and stir in the sugar until completely dissolved. Then place the banana slices in the pan and cook until soft. Stir in the Cointreau. Heat the rum in a ladle or small pan until hot - do not boil - ignite, and pour over the bananas, stirring in until the flames die down. Place a scoop of ice cream in each dish and spoon 4 pieces of banana and some sauce over each one. Serve immediately.

Serves 6

PINA COLADA TAMALES

200g white Masa Harina
100g butter
2 tsp. baking powder
2tsp. light muscovado sugar
40g desiccated coconut
200mls creamy coconut
50mls rum
50mls pineapple juice

Filling
100g raisins
50g butter
50g muscovado sugar
50mls rum
50mls pineapple juice
250g pineapple chunks (fresh or tinned)

In a large bowl mix the Masa Harina, baking powder, sugar and dessicated coconut together. Melt the butter and add to the dried ingredients. Pour in the creamy coconut, rum and pineapple juice and mix into a dough. Set aside and make the filling.

Filling
Melt the butter and stir in the sugar to form a syrup. Add the raisins, pineapple chunks and pineapple juice and simmer for 15-20 minutes until liquid disappears. Stir in the rum and remove from heat.
To assemble the tamales, take sheets of tinfoil approx. 8x12cm and spread a thin layer of dough over, leaving a couple of cms. all the way round the tinfoil. Spread a little of the filling and fold into little parcels, making sure they are sealed at both ends with the tinfoil. Place parcels in the top of a steamer and steam for 45 minutes. Remove from steamer and cool slightly so you don't burn your fingers. Remove tinfoil and serve hot with vanilla ice cream. Delicious!

Makes 10-12 tamales

MISSISSIPPI MUD CAKE

200g plain chocolate (70% cocoa solids)
25g butter

200g butter
200g sugar
qtr. tsp. salt
4 eggs (beaten) 1 tsp. vanilla extract
2 tbsp. dark Karo corn syrup
240g plain flour
50mls sunflower oil

Grease a 9-inch springform pan.

Melt the chocolate and 25g butter together over a low heat. Set aside to cool. Sieve the flour and salt together. Cream the butter and gradually add the sugar beating well after each addition. Pour in the oil and beat until smooth. Add the eggs and beat until fluffy. Stir in the syrup, vanilla extract and cooled chocolate until well combined. Fold in the flour a little at a time, folding well after each addition until all ingredients combine into a smooth cake dough. Pour into the greased pan and bake in a preheated oven at 180°C gas mark 4 for 25-30 minutes or until a toothpick inserted 3 cm from the side comes out clean. This cake is supposed to be very soft in the middle. Delicious served with a big dollop of whipped cream or sour cream.

Serves 10-12

TWO COOKS AND A SUITCASE

Tequila Guide

Tequila Guide

TEQUILA AND MESCAL FACTS

We once stood in the centre of the Church in San Juan Chemula on San Mateo Day. Pine needles lay thick on the floor, their scent combined with the acrid smoke from a thousand candles and incense burners. All around the villagers burped loudly and crossed themselves in the direction of a very anguished looking JC. Along the back wall, drunken men lay unconscious at the foot of their selected saintly statue, faces pressed against the pine needles. Most were clutching empty bottles of Agave liquor. Having burped all the badness from their bodies, the next stage of worship was to render the barriers of the conscious mind obsolete, allowing cleansing spirits access to their inner being.

The people of San Juan Chemula were celebrating their religion the way they have for centuries. Happy, drunk and burping loudly.

Pulque - the original alcoholic drink made from nectar extracted from the Agave Plant. A very basic fermentation process produces this milky, oogy drink. To me, even after the introduction of fresh fruit purée, it still remains undrinkable. Some Mexicans adore the stuff and there's a new rise in popularity and respect for the drink.

Mescal and Tequila - if your only Mescal/Tequila experience involves slamming the cheap stuff with something fizzy at an office party and waking up with the boss's pants on your head, please read on.

Mescal - is the overall term used to describe fermented and distilled Agave nectar. Many regions produce Mescal using any one of a number of Agave plants. The State of Oaxaca produces some amazing results and recent official government bodies have registered certain Mescal producers, guaranteeing a level of quality.

Some producers pop in the legendary Agave worm, partly due to the tradition of proving that the sugar level was correct in the Agave plant at the time of harvest - i.e. the worm feeds when the plant is ready for Mescal production. There is undoubtedly a gimmick element to the worm. With or without it, though, there are some pretty good Mescals out there.

Very Important Fact - the worm has no hallucinogenic properties whatsoever and Mescal has no connection to the drug mescaline. Sorry!

Tequila - In much the same way as Champagne is a very special regional interpretation of fizzy wine, Tequila is a very special regional Mescal. Only Blue Agave is used in the making of Tequila and this must be grown and harvested in one of five nominated regions in Mexico. The production of Tequila has been carefully monitored for many years and each producer is allocated a special NOM number. If this number is not present on the bottle you're not drinking authentic Tequila.

100% Pure Agave - this means that only sugars extracted from the Agave Plant have been used. If this information does not appear on your bottle, you are drinking 51% Agave and 49% something else – cane spirit e.g.

Blanco/Plata - white or silver Tequila that has not been aged.
Reposado - aged 6 months in wooden vats or specially selected barrels.
Añejo - aged 12 months and over in wooden vats or specially selected barrels.
Gold - product containing food colouring.

Dispelling the Myths/Summary

- Tequila is not made from Cactus
- Tequila is made from the Blue Agave Plant
- Tequila does not contain a worm
- Tequila is not hallucinogenic
- Mescal is made from various types of Agave Plant
- Mescal is not related to the drug mescaline
- Mescal sometimes contains a worm
- Peyote is a highly hallucinogenic fungi
- Mescal is not hallucinogenic

HOW TO DRINK TEQUILA

Shot Glasses - your favourite 100% Agave Tequila, a small pinch of salt, wedge of lime.
Method - place salt on your tongue, this will open the pours of your tongue and stimulate your taste buds. Pop in the Tequila, savour and swallow, cleanse mouth with lime.
Brandy Glass - very expensive Reposado and Anejo work very well savoured from brandy glasses.
Two Shot Glass - fill one with your favourite Tequila and the other with Sangrita. Drink sip for sip at your own pace. **Note** - when you finish a glass of Coctel de Camerone (p54) the shrimp flavoured tomato juice makes an excellent Sangrita and should be savoured with a shot of Tequila.

SANGRITA

100ml tomato juice
juice of two oranges
juice of one lime
1 tblsp. Grenadine
1 small onion (chopped fine)
2 Serrano chiles (chopped fine)
salt and pepper to taste
some coriander for garnish

Blend all ingredients, except coriander, in a mixer. Serve well chilled. Garnish each glassfull with chopped coriander.

MARGARITA

2 parts Tequila (100% Agave preferably)
1 part Triple Sec
1 part lime juice (fresh)
ice cubes (for chilling only)
salt for the rim of glass if desired

Rub the rim of the glass with a lime wedge and dip in fine sea salt (salt is optional).
Mix your ingredients in a jug or cocktail shaker. Strain into glasses, leaving the ice to melt in the empty jug, not in your glass. This might seem high in alcohol and low in limejuice, but a good Margarita should be.

SOME DON'TS
Don't drown with lime or you will end up with a dry mouth and an over acid gut.
Don't fill the glass with ice cubes or worse still, crushed ice. The ice melts in the glass and you get a watered down taste experience.